Modern Critical Interpretations

William Faulkner's Sanctuary

Modern Critical Interpretations

These and other titles in preparation

Modern Critical Interpretations

William Faulkner's
Sanctuary

Edited and with an introduction by

Harold Bloom
Sterling Professor of the Humanities
Yale University

1988

AUG

Chelsea House Publishers ◇ *1988*
NEW YORK ◇ NEW HAVEN ◇ PHILADELPHIA

© 1988 by Chelsea House Publishers, a division
of Chelsea House Educational Communications, Inc.

Introduction © 1988 by Harold Bloom

Printed and bound in the United States of America

10 9 8 7 6 5 4 3 2 1

∞ The paper used in this publication meets the minimum
requirements of the American National Standard for
Permanence of Paper for Printed Library Materials, Z39.48–1984

Library of Congress Cataloging-in-Publication Data
William Faulkner's Sanctuary.
    (Modern critical interpretations)
    Bibliography: p.
    Includes index.
    Contents: The function of narrative pattern in
Sanctuary / Joseph W. Reed, Jr.—Sanctuary, from
confrontation to peaceful void / Calvin S. Brown—
Sanctuary and Dostoevsky / Jean Weisgerber—[etc.]
    1. Faulkner, William, 1897–1962.   Sanctuary.
I. Bloom, Harold.   II. Series.
PS3511.A86S4387   1988   813'.52   87–27756
ISBN 1–55546–041–0

Contents

Editor's Note

This book brings together a representative selection of the best critical interpretations of William Faulkner's novel *Sanctuary*. The critical essays are reprinted here in the chronological order of their original publication. I am grateful to Dennis Fawcett and Bruce Covey for their help in editing this volume.

My introduction locates *Sanctuary* in relation to the genealogy of Faulkner's imagination and then centers upon the rhetoric of the opening and the close of the book. Joseph W. Reed, Jr., begins the chronological sequence of criticism with an analysis of the narrative pattern of *Sanctuary,* which he sees as denying us empathy and enforcing coldness, and so is a performance that ignores the audience.

In Calvin S. Brown's reading, the novel is not despairing but rather inhabits the peaceful void of a philosophical nihilism. *Sanctuary's* relation to Dostoevsky's influence is studied by Jean Weisgerber, who finds significant evidence of the effect of *The Brothers Karamazov* upon Faulkner's narrative.

Faulkner's indubitable misogyny is traced through *Sanctuary* by Albert J. Guerard, while Elizabeth M. Kerr shrewdly shows that the work is indeed a very good instance of Gothic fiction. Noel Polk states the case for the first version of *Sanctuary* over the second and argues that the two versions taken together are a composite entity of greater value.

In this book's final essay, Robert R. Moore studies Temple Drake as being her own victim, trapped in the sanctuary of her own solipsism.

Introduction

I

No critic need invent William Faulkner's obsessions with what Nietzsche might have called the genealogy of the imagination. Recent critics of Faulkner, including David Minter, John T. Irwin, David M. Wyatt, and Richard H. King, have emphasized the novelist's profound need to believe himself to have been his own father, in order to escape not only the Freudian family romance and literary anxieties of influence, but also the cultural dilemmas of what King terms "the Southern family romance." From *The Sound and the Fury* through the debacle of *A Fable,* Faulkner centers upon the sorrows of fathers and sons, to the disadvantage of mothers and daughters. No feminist critic ever will be happy with Faulkner. His brooding conviction that female sexuality is closely allied with death seems essential to all of his strongest fictions. It may even be that Faulkner's rhetorical economy, his wounded need to get his cosmos into a single sentence, is related to his fear that origin and end might prove to be one. Nietzsche prophetically had warned that origin and end were separate entities, and for the sake of life had to be kept apart, but Faulkner (strangely like Freud) seems to have known that the only Western trope participating neither in origin nor end is the image of the father.

By universal consent of critics and common readers, Faulkner now is recognized as the strongest American novelist of this century, clearly surpassing Hemingway and Fitzgerald, and standing as an equal in the sequence that includes Hawthorne, Melville, Mark Twain, and Henry James. Some critics might add Dreiser to this group; Faulkner himself curiously would have insisted upon Thomas Wolfe, a generous though dubious judgment. The American precur-

1

sor for Faulkner was Sherwood Anderson, but perhaps only as an impetus; the true American forerunner is the poetry of T. S. Eliot, as Judith L. Sensibar demonstrates. But the truer precursor for Faulkner's fiction is Conrad, inescapable for the American novelists of Faulkner's generation, including Hemingway and Fitzgerald. Comparison to Conrad is dangerous for any novelist, and clearly Faulkner did not achieve a *Nostromo*. But his work of the decade 1929–39 does include four permanent books: *The Sound and the Fury, As I Lay Dying, Light in August,* and *Absalom, Absalom!* If one adds *Sanctuary* and *The Wild Palms,* and *The Hamlet* and *Go Down, Moses* in the early forties, then the combined effect is extraordinary.

From Malcolm Cowley on, critics have explained this effect as the consequence of the force of mythmaking, at once personal and local. Cleanth Brooks, the rugged final champion of the New Criticism, essentially reads Faulkner as he does Eliot's *The Waste Land,* finding the hidden God of the normative Christian tradition to be the basis for Faulkner's attitude towards nature. Since Brooks calls Faulkner's stance Wordsworthian, and finds Wordsworthian nature a Christian vision also, the judgment involved necessarily has its problematical elements. Walter Pater, a critic in a very different tradition, portrayed a very different Wordsworth in terms that seem to me not inapplicable to Faulkner:

> Religious sentiment, consecrating the affections and natu-
> ral regrets of the human heart, above all, that pitiful awe
> and care for the perishing human clay, of which relic-
> worship is but the corruption, has always had much to do
> with localities, with the thoughts which attach themselves
> to actual scenes and places. Now what is true of it
> everywhere, is truest of it in those secluded valleys where
> one generation after another maintains the same abiding
> place; and it was on this side, that Wordsworth appre-
> hended religion most strongly. Consisting, as it did so
> much, in the recognition of local sanctities, in the habit of
> connecting the stones and trees of a particular spot of earth
> with the great events of life, till the low walls, the green
> mounds, the half-obliterated epitaphs seemed full of
> voices, and a sort of natural oracles, the very religion of
> those people of the dales, appeared but as another link

between them and the earth, and was literally a religion of nature.

A kind of stoic natural religion pervades this description, something close to the implicit faith of old Isaac McCaslin in *Go Down, Moses*. It seems unhelpful to speak of "residual Christianity" in Faulkner, as Cleanth Brooks does. Hemingway and Fitzgerald, in their nostalgias, perhaps were closer to a Christian ethos than Faulkner was in his great phase. Against current critical judgment, I prefer *As I Lay Dying* and *Light in August* to *The Sound and the Fury* and *Absalom, Absalom!*, partly because the first two are more primordial in their vision, closer to the stoic intensities of their author's kind of natural piety. There is an *otherness* in Lena Grove and the Bundrens that would have moved Wordsworth, that is, the Wordsworth of *The Tale of Margaret, Michael,* and *The Old Cumberland Beggar*. A curious movement that is also a stasis becomes Faulkner's pervasive trope for Lena. Though he invokes the imagery of Keats's urn, Faulkner seems to have had the harvest-girl of Keats's *To Autumn* more in mind, or even the stately figures of the *Ode on Indolence*. We remember Lena Grove as stately, calm, a person yet a process, a serene and patient consciousness, full of wonder, too much a unitary being to need even her author's variety of stoic courage.

The uncanniness of this representation is exceeded by the Bundrens, whose plagency testifies to Faulkner's finest rhetorical achievement. *As I Lay Dying* may be the most original novel ever written by an American. Obviously it is not free of the deepest influence Faulkner knew as a novelist. The language is never Conradian, and yet the sense of the reality principle is. But there is nothing in Conrad like Darl Bundren, not even in *The Secret Agent*. *As I Lay Dying* is Faulkner's strongest protest against the facticity of literary convention, against the force of the familial past, which tropes itself in fiction as the repetitive form of narrative imitating prior narrative. The book is a sustained nightmare, insofar as it is Darl's book, which is to say, Faulkner's book, or the book of his daemon.

II

Canonization is a process of enshrining creative misinterpretations, and no one need lament this. Still, one element that ensues from this process all too frequently is the not very creative misinterpretation in which the idiosyncratic is distorted into the normative. Churchwardenly critics who assimilate the Faulkner of the thirties to spiritual, social, and moral orthodoxy can and do assert Faulkner himself as their preceptor. But this is the Faulkner of the fifties, Nobel laureate, State Department envoy, and author of *A Fable,* a book of a badness simply astonishing for Faulkner. The best of the normative critics, Cleanth Brooks, reads even *As I Lay Dying* as a quest for community, an exaltation of the family, an affirmation of Christian values. The Bundrens manifestly constitute one of the most terrifying visions of the family romance in the history of literature. But their extremism is not eccentric in the 1929–39 world of Faulkner's fiction. That world is founded upon a horror of families, a limbo of outcasts, an evasion of all values other than stoic endurance. It is a world in which what is silent in the other Bundrens speaks in Darl, what is veiled in the Compsons is uncovered in Quentin. So tangled are these returns of the repressed with what continues to be estranged that phrases like "the violation of the natural" and "the denial of the human" become quite meaningless when applied to Faulkner's greater fictions. In that world, the natural is itself a violation and the human already a denial. Is the weird quest of the Bundrens a violation of the natural, or is it what Blake would have called a terrible triumph for the selfish virtues of the natural heart? Darl judges it to be the latter, but Darl luminously denies the sufficiency of the human, at the cost of what seems schizophrenia.

Marxist criticism of imaginative literature, if it had not regressed abominably in our country, so that now it is a travesty of the dialectical suppleness of Adorno and Benjamin, would find a proper subject in the difficult relationship between the 1929 business panic and *As I Lay Dying.* Perhaps the self-destruction of our delusive political economy helped free Faulkner from whatever inhibitions, communal and personal, had kept him earlier from a saga like that of the Bundrens. Only an authentic seer can give permanent form to a prophecy like *As I Lay Dying,* which puts severely into question every received notion we have of the natural and the human. Darl asserts he has no mother, while taunting his enemy brother, Jewel, with the insistence that Jewel's mother was a horse. Their little brother, Vardaman, says: "My mother is a fish." The mother, dead and undead, is uncannier even than these children, when she confesses the truth of her existence, her rejecting vision of her children:

> I could just remember how my father used to say that the reason for living was to get ready to stay dead a long time. And when I would have to look at them day after day, each with his and her single and selfish thought, and blood strange to each other blood and strange to mine, and think that this seemed to be the only way I could get ready to stay dead, I would hate my father for having ever planted me. I would look forward to the times when they faulted, so I could whip them. When the switch fell I could feel it upon my flesh; when it welted and ridged it was my blood that ran, and I would think with each blow of the switch: Now you are aware of me! Now I am something in your secret and selfish life, who have marked your blood with my own for ever and ever.

This veritable apocalypse of any sense of otherness is no mere "denial of community." Nor are the Bundrens any "mimesis of essential nature." They are a super-mimesis, an over-representation mocking nature while shadowing it. What matters in major Faulkner is that the people have gone back, not to nature but to some abyss before the Creation-Fall. Eliot insisted that Joyce's imagination was eminently orthodox. This can be doubted, but in Faulkner's case there is little sense in baptizing his imagination. One sees why he preferred reading the Old Testament to the New, remarking that the former was stories and the latter, ideas. The remark is inadequate except insofar as it opposes Hebraic to Hellenistic representation of character. There is little that is Homeric about the Bundrens, or Sophoclean about the Compsons. Faulkner's irony is neither classical nor romantic, neither Greek nor German. It does not say one thing while meaning another, nor trade in contrasts between expectation and fulfillment. Instead, it juxtaposes incommensurable realities: of self and other, of parent and child, of past and future. When Gide maintained that Faulkner's people lacked souls, he simply failed to observe that Faulkner's ironies were biblical. To which an amendment must be added. In Faulkner, only the ironies are biblical. What Faulkner's people lack is the blessing; they cannot contend for a time without boundaries. Yahweh will make no covenant with them. Their agon therefore is neither the Greek one for the foremost place nor the Hebrew one for the blessing, which honors the father and the mother. Their agon is the hopeless one of waiting for their doom to lift.

III

In *Sanctuary*, no one even bothers to wait for doom to lift; the novel is as nihilistic as John Webster's *The White Devil* or Cyril Tourneur's *The Atheist's Tragedy*. Malraux asserted that Greek tragedy entered the detective story in *Sanctuary*. Had Malraux spoken of Jacobean tragedy, his remarks would have been to some purpose. Though directly influenced by Conrad and Dostoevsky, *Sanctuary* comes closer to Webster and Tourneur than T. S. Eliot does, even when he explicitly imitates them. Robert Penn Warren, much under Faulkner's influence (and Eliot's), is the other modern writer who unmistakably reminds us of the Jacobeans. Tragic farce is the true Jacobean mode, and the mixed genre of *Sanctuary*—Gothic thriller, detective and gangster story, shocker, entertainment—quite accurately can be termed tragic farce.

Sanctuary is the enigma among Faulkner's novels; intended as a potboiler and moneymaker, it very nearly achieves major status and can sustain many rereadings. Its protagonists, like Webster's, designedly resist psychologizing. *Sanctuary*'s extraordinary humor and what might be called a grotesque assortment of eloquences in Faulkner's rhetoric, high and low, combine to keep the book alive in the memory of the reader. Famous passages at its start and its conclusion remain remarkable as epiphanies—Paterian, Conradian, Joycean—in which spiritual realities flare forth against mundane backgrounds. Here is the novel's opening:

> From beyond the screen of bushes which surrounded the spring, Popeye watched the man drinking. A faint path led from the road to the spring. Popeye watched the man—a tall, thin man, hatless, in worn gray flannel trousers and carrying a tweed coat over his arm—emerge from the path and kneel to drink from the spring.
>
> The spring welled up at the root of a beech tree and flowed away upon a bottom of whorled and waved sand. It was surrounded by a thick growth of cane and brier, of cypress and gum in which broken sunlight lay sourceless.

Somewhere, hidden and secret yet nearby, a bird sang three notes and ceased.

In the spring the drinking man leaned his face to the broken and myriad reflection of his own drinking. When he rose up he saw among them the shattered reflection of Popeye's straw hat, though he had heard no sound.

He saw, facing him across the spring, a man of under size, his hands in his coat pockets, a cigarette slanted from his chin. His suit was black, with a tight, high-waisted coat. His trousers were rolled once and caked with mud above mud-caked shoes. His face had a queer, bloodless color, as though seen by electric light; against the sunny silence, in his slanted straw hat and his slightly akimbo arms, he had that vicious depthless quality of stamped tin.

Behind him the bird sang again, three bars in monotonous repetition: a sound meaningless and profound out of a suspirant and peaceful following silence which seemed to isolate the spot, and out of which a moment later came the sound of an automobile passing along a road and dying away.

No reader is going to become at ease with Popeye (Faulkner thought him a monster, but sympathized with him anyway) and no reader forgets him either. I recall Faulkner's observation somewhere that his Popeye, in the movies, ought to be played by Mickey Mouse, a rather more amiable cartoon than Popeye constitutes. Popeye is nightmare, as this opening passage conveys; he is a phantasmagoria of flesh illuminated by electric light, a two-dimensional figure stamped out of tin. We are not surprised that his sexual organ pragmatically should be a corncob, or that he passively allows himself to be executed at the book's close. He represents not a dualism, whether Platonic or Freudian, but a monistic nihilism, a machine uninhabited by a ghost. The bird, singing from its hidden and secret recess nearby, is part of that nihilism, "in monotonous repetition: a sound meaningless and profound." Perhaps by way of Eliot's *The Waste Land*, Faulkner returns us to the great American trope of a hidden bird singing from a dark and secret place in a swamp, Whitman's hermit thrush in *When Lilacs Last in the Dooryard Bloom'd*. Whitman's bird sang a song of sane and sacred death; the bird of Popeye's epiphany might as well be a clock, sounding the repetitions for death in *Sanctuary*, insane and obscene death.

The impressionism of *Sanctuary* derives from Conrad, almost as though *Sanctuary* is Conrad's *Chance* gone mad. *Sanctuary* will not sustain aesthetic comparison with Conrad's *The Secret Agent*, but there are spiritual and structural affinities between the two novels. Faulkner's detachment in *Sanctuary* is astonishing and empties out the book with high deliberateness. Against Cleanth Brooks, I must assert that there is no Vision of Evil in *Sanctuary*. A narrative whose central protagonists are Popeye and Temple Drake, not Horace Benbow and Ruby Lamar, knows itself too well to desire any pandering to moral judgments. Popeye is a mechanical jack-in-the-box; Temple ends as a mechanical figurine in *Sanctuary*'s concluding passage:

> It had been a gray day, a gray summer, a gray year. On the street old men wore overcoats, and in the Luxembourg Gardens as Temple and her father passed the women sat knitting in shawls and even the men playing croquet played in coats and capes, and in the sad gloom of the chestnut trees the dry click of balls, the random shouts of children, had that quality of autumn, gallant and evanescent and forlorn. From beyond the circle with its spurious Greek balustrade, clotted with movement, filled with a gray light of the same color and texture as the water which the fountain played into the pool, came a steady crash of music. They went on, passed the pool where the children and an old man in a shabby brown overcoat sailed toy boats, and entered the trees again and found seats. Immediately an old woman came with decrepit promptitude and collected four sous.
>
> In the pavilion a band in the horizon blue of the army played Massenet and Scriabine, and Berlioz like a thin coating of tortured Tschaikovsky on a slice of stale bread, while the twilight dissolved in wet gleams from the branches, onto the pavilion and the sombre toadstools of umbrellas. Rich and resonant the brasses crashed and died in the thick green twilight, rolling over them in rich sad waves. Temple yawned behind her hand, then she took out a compact and opened it upon a face in miniature sullen

and discontented and sad. Beside her her father sat, his hands crossed on the head of his stick, the rigid bar of his moustache beaded with moisture like frosted silver. She closed the compact and from beneath her smart new hat she seemed to follow with her eyes the waves of music, to dissolve into the dying brasses, across the pool and the opposite semicircle of trees where at sombre intervals the dead tranquil queens in stained marble mused, and on into the sky lying prone and vanquished in the embrace of the season of rain and death.

This high rhetoric is as much a failure as the book's opening passage was a success. Faulkner, self-consciously invading the ambiance of Hemingway and Fitzgerald, is anxious and over-writes. He ought to have ended *Sanctuary* with the hanging of Popeye, affectless and economical. We are embarrassed by that "sky lying prone and vanquished in the embrace of the season of rain and death," partly because the sky there is a trope substituting for the violated sanctuary of Temple's body. *Sanctuary* does not share the strength of Faulkner's best work, *As I Lay Dying* and *Light in August,* but I perversely prefer it to *The Sound and the Fury* and *Absalom, Absalom!* It lacks their aspirations and their pretensions, and may in time seem a more original work than either. Its uneven and conflicting rhetorics wound it, but it survives as narrative and as fearsome image, still representative of American realities after more than a half-century.

The Function of Narrative Pattern in *Sanctuary*

Joseph W. Reed, Jr.

> To me it is a cheap idea, because it was deliberately
> conceived to make money. . . . I tore the galleys down
> and rewrote the book. It had been already set up once, so
> I had to pay for the privilege of rewriting it, trying to
> make out of it something which would not shame *The
> Sound and the Fury* and *As I Lay Dying* too much and I
> made a fair job and I hope you will buy it and tell your
> friends and I hope they will buy it too.
>
> (1932 introduction to Sanctuary)

Faulkner's statement in the introduction to the Modern Library issue
of *Sanctuary* is an apologia. He indicates a tension between temptation
and duty: "a cheap idea" had to be made into "something which
would not shame" his work. The novel itself perhaps falls between
stools in much the same way, but it falls with a bang, triumphantly
true to that tension and consequently true to itself alone. It is no
more written with the left hand than Graham Greene's "entertain-
ments" are. Behind the dirty leer of the persona he has adopted for
the introduction is still Faulkner, telling a story, planning effects,
and, in this phase of his career, spending most of the time calculating
technique.

From *Faulkner's Narrative*. © 1973 by Yale University. Yale University Press, 1973.

The "cheap idea" is undeniably there. The substance of the book is chosen for sensational shock. But Faulkner in an interview identified sensationalism as secondary.

> I would say, if he is creating characters which are flesh-and-blood people, are believable, and are honest and true, then he can use sensationalism if he thinks that's an effective way to tell his story. But if he's writing just for sensationalism, then he has betrayed his vocation, and he deserves to suffer from it. That is, sensationalism is in a way an incidental tool, that he might use sensationalism as the carpenter picks up another hammer to drive a nail. But he doesn't—the carpenter don't build a house just to drive nails. He drives nails to build a house.

Here, quite literally, the objects of the book—the corncob, the cosmetician's plug of wax which pops out of the hole in Red's forehead, the two lovebirds cut up with the scissors and the half-grown kitten, even Popeye himself, an object fashioned of stamped tin, old auto parts, and a cigarette—are the raw materials which challenge Faulkner's technique to combine them in such a way that they will not "shame." His response to the challenge is a mixed narrative which explores not just the uses of sensational objects but of narrative techniques usually thought of as "cheap," techniques which emulate and imitate various patterns drawn from popular media and the oral tradition. But the disciplined stylistic and narrative control which unifies the mixture of imitations and the complex, multilevel structure are rather expensive ideas. Quite apparently money alone was not a good enough reason to write the book, in spite of the gallus-snapping, hard-bellied persona of the introduction. What began as a cheap idea did not emerge as a cheap book. *Sanctuary* cannot be dismissed as a potboiler. But its simple (or cheap) origins, its chronological place, and the overtness of its strategy make it ideal as a starting point for an examination of the function of narrative pattern in the novels.

Leslie Fiedler holds that the book is not just the "darkest of all Faulkner's books" but "the dirtiest of all the dirty jokes exchanged among men only at the expense of the abdicating Anglo-Saxon virgin." Either Fiedler hasn't paid much attention to the jokes he's heard or he's heard pretty bad ones, because the book fails in just this respect: it will not become pornography and its generic structure refuses to conform to that of the dirty joke. Certainly the corncob, the corncrib, elements of Tommy and the deaf-and-blind old man emerge from the same great mass of popular oral material as the hillbilly jokes of the twenties and thirties (perhaps most concretely remembered in the old *Esquire* hillbilly cartoons or in the gradeschool ditty, "We Mountaineers, we have no fears"), that vein Erskine Caldwell mined so tirelessly. But again these are objects rather than stories. In technique, only chapter 21, the tale of Virgil Snopes and Fonzo, fits the pattern of the dirty joke, but even it omits the punchline. The novel is not so relentlessly directed as a dirty joke must be, in which everything must be constructed to serve the climax. There are elements of that strangely antijoke form of joke, the shaggy-dog story, in Temple's wanderings about the farm, but even shaggy-dogs must have a punchline, and this has none, unless it is the corncob, so carefully put off for fourteen chapters and 220 pages until it can be introduced in evidence at the trial. The pursuit of Temple fits more surely into the genre of the euphemistic semipornography of pulp fiction of the twenties and thirties, teasing and teasing up to an encounter, and then throwing in a lot of colorful writing for the "Afterwards as they lay together" section. Here again it is a truncated imitation, for the tease is surely there, but we are led to an encounter and then denied it, and even the "afterwards" is delayed. As dirty joke or as pornography, *Sanctuary* is like another feature of the Japanese sex manual printed on tissue paper. Male and female figures can be superimposed one on the other, but it's not printed dirty—you make it dirty yourself.

The humor in the semipornographic imitation of pulp is the humor of excess, the nervous laughter of Grand Guignol or effective melodrama. This contrasts with another kind of humor in the book, the high-class one-liners of Miss Jenny's scenes. The world Horace re-enters in chapter 3 is that of high drawing-room comedy. Jokes may be made about lack of manhood, but they are in the vein of *The Country Wife,* not the Travelling Salesman. Miss Jenny perhaps reaches her highest point of successful and witty—but inhumanly distant—commentary on the lowlife of the present by another device of Restoration wit: using the past as a weapon to beat the mores of the present with. The present somehow threatens to soil her. And we discover in the process of the book that this is a true threat. She maintains the only position of true safety in the world of *Sanctuary*.

Experiments in imitation and emulation go beyond structural and narrative similarity into a combination of character-cliché, situation, and narrative technique. Here and there is an unmistakable odor of old newsprint, a suggestion of tabloid journalism which finally comes to full force in chapter 31, the story of Popeye. Its form is as old as journalism itself—the formative years or the confessions of the condemned criminal, a form which has changed little between the *Newgate Calendar* and the current copy of *Midnight*.

The dancehall sequence before Red is killed, Temple's ride into Memphis, and some of Ruby's autobiographical narration of her loyalty to Lee are so strongly redolent of popcorn and gummy folding seats that there can be no mistaking either the atmosphere which holds the vision or the cliché counterparts for the characters— flaming youth at the dancehall, the tart with the heart-of-gold, the moll faithful to the end outside the walls of Sing Sing Prison—all come from Hollywood. Perhaps this is why in spite of sleazy adaptation the second film of *Sanctuary* had moments of power. Even if Popeye is transposed into a devilishly attractive Candyman in Yves Montand and the whole movie is an insult even to *Sanctuary,* all the film clichés are there set down in order, and the book's movie must coalesce here and there with the movie's movie. Some of the passages which seem to have been clipped from second features could not, of course, have been done by Hollywood of the late twenties, even though movie censorship had not yet become very forceful. These must be credited again to a source common to both, pulp fiction. The somewhat antiquarian sensationalism of too much alcohol and lost women on a steady diet of gin is rather thin stuff for the appetite of a sensationalist of the sixties or seventies, but these and white slavery—all calculated forty years ago to produce a shock in us as readers which we can't quite manage any more—emerge from the backgrounds of cheap fiction and its high moralistic tone. It's possible that the aging decline of the book's shock value in the years since publication has made it possible for us to see the design more clearly. Now that we can no longer dismiss it with confidence as Faulkner's dirty book, we can no longer accept Faulkner's claim for it as a "cheap idea."

It is as American as apple pie and as violent as it is American. But not all of this Americanism is simple imitation in "period" manner. One of its imitational forebears moves beyond contemporaneous life to a much deeper and perhaps even more useful source of violent narrative. The land is hostile and there are Indians here, bent on their own odd designs, weird rites, and curious religious practices. The similarity to narratives of Indian captivity is apparent when the book is compared to "Red Leaves," and Temple is put in the place of the black bodyservant of that story in her cultural contrast to her captors, in her pursuit, in her peculiar helplessness. She has nothing to do with their aims, but she has stumbled among them and is now subject to their laws and customs. The pattern is even clearer if Temple is compared to women of the early captivity narratives. Among the Indians the captive first sees her captors as devils; then sees them become evil men and finally they become mere functions of their alien society. Popeye's development from his early mono-syllabic replies through his comparatively garrulous responses in Memphis to the almost humanizing explanation for his evil in genetic and environmental abnormality (chap. 31) parallels this. Captivity can include a process in which the captive passes through cultural shock into an adjustment of his values to those of the alien society, almost acceptance and liking (a friendly squaw like Ruby, a change in one or another devil into something human), and then becomes, in turn, alienated from his own society. The process must end in self-condemnation in the narrative of Indian captivity, espe-cially under the Puritan ethos of the parent society. The captive was a sinner when she was captured (because she was a good Christian woman, and all good Christian women are self-accused sinners), she was brought to captivity for her sins, while in captivity she sinned more (by adapting herself to the company of the godless heathen), so that after her rescue she looks back upon her behavior in captivity with mixed feelings which can result in a misanthropy similar to the disaffection for humans Lemuel Gulliver felt in order to justify his affection for Houyhnhnms. There was a corresponding condemna-tion of her by her native society and suspicion or even accusation of cohabitation with the savages.

In *Sanctuary* the judging function of the Puritan ethic is sup-planted by several sets of standards against which Temple may be judged—the tone of moral indignation transplanted from pulp fiction, the disapproval of the Miss Jennys of the world of Jefferson or of the society of "respectability" which her father the judge represents. The structure of captivity narratives can fall, as in *Sanctuary*, into two parts: the capture and the adventures and adjustments in captivity, and the sometimes parallel narrative of the beginning and execution of the rescue process. The full pattern of cultural assimilation, alienation from her own society, and disaffection is only completed in *Requiem for a Nun,* but the tensions unresolved in Temple here are strikingly similar to those of the original captives.

Sanctuary, then, moves in patterns borrowed from both deep and shallow sources: from the deep, a pattern of mounting terror first at the fact of captivity, then at the failure to try to escape. Running parallel to this is the arbitrary, hard-edged, nervous quality of tabloid journalism in some parts and pulp-fiction in others, directness which makes no apology for its literary forebears, overt imitation which cultivates the appearance and effect of unrefined arrangement and unpolished contrast. From second-feature movies come the isolation of the observing eye—its distance from human concern—the arbitrary sequence, the harsh lighting, the black-and-white, third-person objective qualities. In combination, all of these make up a narrative which may be ridiculed while it is being read, and which certainly never measures up to Faulkner's work at the top of his form, but which rests in the memory more securely in the manner of powerful myth than does any of his other works.

Why it falls short of the novels of the main range is more difficult to resolve. Why does such careful calculation and skillful pastiche fail to satisfy as one reads along? I think it is because Faulkner breaks one of his own rules in this book. *Sanctuary* is calculated to serve the reader, both in individual effect and in driving narrative impetus, but in *Sanctuary* Faulkner was willing to sacrifice total entertainment—his central aim in pleasing the Hearer—in order to please himself with harsh impact and unrelieved hopelessness. The book carries us along and delivers sometimes more than it promises; but it refuses to satisfy our need and desire for a place to stand, an undamaged ideal, even a hint of the hope of human efficacy. There is no Ishmael, and *Sanctuary* as a result is more of an object like Popeye than it is an experience shared.

The book is moved by almost objective contrasts. The narrative is split between the enclave and the town, Frenchman's Bend–Memphis and Jefferson, the captors and the captivity, and the rescuers' success and failure. The division is made sharply by chapters: Frenchman's Bend–Memphis in chapters 1–2, 4–14, 18, 21, 24–25, 31; and Jefferson in chapters 3, 15–17, 19–20, 26–30. The parts of each are continuous from the end of one section to the beginning of the next, with convergences of the two narrative lines in chapters 1–2, 23, and 27. The arrangement has the force and impetus of a tight end-plotted nineteenth-century novel, with its immediate transitions and an almost creaky overtness of device. It is a powerful but strongly artificial structure.

But within this simple and rather blunt general structure there is great variation of effect. Neither of the two lines is stylistically continuous: rather the immediate material at hand determines the immediate treatment for each section. Chapters 1 and 2 balance a nightmare world with an obliviously self-indulgent Horace and introduce the oddly indifferent element of Nature which becomes so important to the moral structure of *Sanctuary*'s world. Chapter 3 returns to Jefferson, Horace assumes his normal role (without the nightmare manner and the loquacious confessions of chapters 1–2), and Faulkner's chronicling manner, the *Sartoris* style, takes over. Basic relationships are set forth in the tracing of Horace's dead-level normalcy. Temple's nightmare, chapters 4–14, is marked by a rigid control of diction and by a dreamy, seemingly pointless wandering about of the characters. Theme and rendering weave in and out of this. The switches between one point of view and another and the switches between point of view and objective omniscience are frequent, apparently ruled by the same arbitrary lack of aim as is Temple herself. Then back in the world of the rescuers (chaps. 15–27) we see the less safe and secluded precincts of society, the operations of the law and order necessary to support chapter 3's aura of comfort and seclusion. The town, the crowds, the functions of society here contrast with the oblivious heaven-tree. Back with captivity at the whorehouse, chapter 28 switches into cinematic, swift narrative and tangible effects. Popeye, once out of Frenchman's Bend, becomes more of a character and necessarily more of a human being. But Faulkner wants it both ways: the world of the whore-house must be shown to be depraved because he is counting on that old shock value of white slavery and too much gin; but the tone of these chapters insists as strongly that they are the affectionate memoir of a closed society, humanizing the necessary evil in their character-ization. There is a glimpse of Oxford (and another tonal and stylistic shift) in chapters 19–20. The dirty joke (21) of Fonzo and Virgil ties ends together too—the pair enforces both the affectionate memoir in their humor and the white slavery wickedness in their innocence— and manages to get us back to Temple. Then the mixture of Snopes's low comedy and Horace's tension between two worlds and chapter 22 returns to the death-row romanticism introduced in the heaven-tree. The first person is dominant in chapter 23; back at the whorehouse, chapters 24–25 return to the cinematic for the death of Red; chapter 26 returns to the town's ineffectual, wandering crowds; chapters 27–28 are Perry Mason. The town and Horace are contrasted in chapter 29, a contrast embodied in the sudden climax of the lynching of Lee, but chapter 30 returns to the *Sartoris* style of chapter 3. Chapter 31 is the tabloid treatment of Popeye, saying more than it tells but explaining less, sharply shifting at the end into a Jamesian mode for Temple in the Luxembourg Gardens.

The overwhelming impression is mixture rather than harmony in the combined movements of the two narrative lines. Nature, in loving and sometimes fulsome description, contributes to this confusion. The descriptive passages seem almost independent of the narrative which surrounds them, and so invite the reader to make them into a pattern or a comment upon the human events they watch over. Almost every section of the book has such a passage, with certain significant exceptions. As sun sets at Frenchman's Bend, Nature disappears, not to reappear until the following morning (chaps. 7–10). It disappears again from the chapters which relate the rape in the corncrib and the departure for Memphis (chaps. 13–14) and again for Red's funeral and the chapter on the prosecutor and Temple's testimony (chaps. 25–28).

The book's opening description introduces Nature's complexity of functions.

> The spring welled up at the root of a beech tree and flowed away upon a bottom of whorled and waved sand. It was surrounded by a thick growth of cane and brier, of cypress and gum in which broken sunlight lay sourceless. Somewhere, hidden and secret yet nearby, a bird sang three notes and ceased.

There is more here than visual background. The undisturbed quality of the sand and woods suggests pastoral, but the sourceless sunlight is a neutral, rather ominous note. The bird is more ominous than neutral. If we pursue that bird in a few more passages it becomes more puzzling than ominous:

> The bird sang again, three bars in monotonous repetition: a sound meaningless and profound out of a suspirant and peaceful following silence which seemed to isolate the spot, and out of which a moment later came the sound of an automobile passing along a road and dying away.

> Now and then the bird sang back in the swamp, as though it were worked by a clock; twice more invisible automobiles passed along the highroad and died away. Again the bird sang.

> Benbow heard the bird again, trying to recall the local name for it. On the invisible highroad another car passed, died away. Between them and the sound of it the sun was almost gone.

> Popeye went on, with light, finicking sounds in the underbrush. Then they ceased. Somewhere in the swamp a bird sang.

Once the bird seems worked by machine, but bird and machine are equally present and ominous and equally neutral. Nature surrounds human actions but keeps its distance. The isolation which either sound provides is clearly now not the isolation of pastoral but rather of false pastoral, less a purifying return to nature than a terrifying distance from anything to which one can call for help.

Neutrality gives way to threat as the book proceeds. Both at Frenchman's Bend and in Jefferson architecture or trees are continually drawn up in silhouette against the sky. This is still neutral, flat, featureless, but it seems to threaten enclosure—something of the threat inherent in expressionist stage decor, the psychological threat of exaggerated height.

Popeye's fear of the woods, of trees, his terror at the owl, all hold out hope that a natural adversary will appear to confront his machine monstrosity. But this is sucker-bait. The natural landscape, from the very outset, takes on attitudes and poses, but continually denies our hopes for any natural solution to anything.

> The slain flowers, the delicate dead flowers and tears.

> That country. Flat and rich and foul, so that the very winds seem to engender money out of it. Like you wouldn't be surprised to find that you could turn in

the leaves off the trees, into the banks for cash. That Delta.

Above the cedar grove beyond whose black interstices an apple orchard flaunted in the sunny afternoon. . . . In a sombre grove through which the breeze drew with a sad, murmurous sound.

Beyond, she could see a weed-choked slope and a huge barn, broken-backed, tranquil in sunny desolation.

Between the sombre spacing of the cedars the orchard lay bright in the sunlight. . . . She walked right through the barn. It was open at the back, upon a mass of jimson weed in savage white-and-lavender bloom. . . . Then she began to run, . . . the weeds slashing at her with huge, moist, malodorous blossoms.

Out of the high darkness where the ragged shadow of the heaven-tree which snooded the street lamp at the corner fretted and mourned.

The outer darkness peaceful with insects and frogs yet filled too with Popeye's presence in black and nameless threat.

The splotched shadow of the heaven-tree shuddered and pulsed monstrously in scarce any wind.

The last trumpet-shape bloom had fallen. . . . They lay thick, viscid underfoot, sweet and oversweet in the nostrils with a sweetness surfeitive and moribund, and at night now the ragged shadow of full-fledged leaves pulsed upon the barred window in shabby rise and fall.

The ragged grief of the heaven tree would pulse and change, the last bloom fallen now in viscid smears upon the sidewalk.

A narrow street of smoke-grimed frame houses . . . set a little back in grassless plots, with now and then a forlorn and hardy tree of some shabby species—gaunt, lopbranched magnolias, a stunted elm or a locust in grayish, cadaverous bloom—interspersed by rear ends of garages.

Fecund, somber, sad, tranquil, savage, malodorous, peaceful, it flaunts, frets, mourns, pulses monstrously, depicts ragged grief, is forlorn, hardy, stunted, cadaverous. It is neither Eden nor Arcadia but rather a self-dramatizing, self-indulgent, helpless hodge-podge of pathetic attitudes, incapable of helping anything or anyone. It overdramatizes itself and its surroundings and does nothing. It is neither the maimed wilderness familiar from Faulkner's favorite theme of human nature's destructiveness, nor is it an ironically sunny backdrop for man's failure at natural dignity. It can slash out or mourn, it can perform a dazzling series of emotional impersonations, but these mean less than its impotent omnipresence. It is there. It sits. It watches. But it is intent only upon its own cycles and survival, its own strange and distant melodrama, not upon anything human going on against it, beneath it, or nearby. It is powerless to comment on anything but itself, and even these comments fail in self-consistency. The impotence is most clearly established in two passages at the center of Temple's ride to Memphis.

> She sat limp in the corner of the seat, watching the steady backward rush of the land—pines in opening vistas splashed with fading dogwood; sedge; fields green with new cotton and empty of any movement, peaceful, as though Sunday were a quality of atmosphere, of light and shade—sitting with her legs close together, listening to the hot minute seeping of her blood, saying dully to herself, I'm still bleeding. I'm still bleeding.

> It was a bright, soft day, a wanton morning filled with that unbelievable soft radiance of May, rife with a promise of noon and of heat, with high fat clouds like gobs of whipped cream floating lightly as reflections in a mirror, their shadows scudding sedately across the road. It had been a lavender spring. The fruit trees, the white ones, had been in small leaf when the blooms matured; they had never attained that brilliant whiteness of last spring, and the dogwood had come into full bloom after the leaf also, in green retrograde before crescendo. But lilac and wistaria and redbud, even the shabby heaven-trees, had never been finer, fulgent, with a burning scent blowing for a hundred yards along the vagrant air of April and May. The bougainvillea against the veranda would be large as bas-

ketballs and lightly poised as balloons, and looking vacantly and stupidly at the rushing roadside Temple began
to scream.

The indifferent neutrality of nature is enforced by the transformation of the city. We might expect a Popeye-city filled with
monstrous grotesques. What we get has some elements of machine-
change horror, but for all that it is happier than we anticipate (or
would hope for if we were trying to construct an allegory of the
machine versus nature). There is an almost transcendent quality of
the magical:

> a low doored cavern of an equivocal appearance where an
> oilcloth-covered counter and a row of backless stools, a
> metal coffee-urn and a fat man in a dirty apron with a
> toothpick in his mouth, stood for an instant out of the
> gloom with an effect as of a sinister and meaningless
> photograph poorly made. From the bluff, beyond a line of
> office buildings terraced sharply against the sun-filled sky,
> came a sound of traffic—motor horns, trolleys—passing
> high overhead on the river breeze; at the end of the street
> a trolley materialised in the narrow gap with an effect as of
> magic and vanished with a stupendous clatter.

> They could hear the city, evocative and strange, imminent
> and remote; threat and promise both—a deep, steady
> sound upon which invisible lights glittered and wavered:
> colored coiling shapes of splendor in which already women
> were beginning to move in suave attitudes of new delights
> and strange nostalgic promises. Fonzo thought of himself
> surrounded by tier upon tier of drawn shades, rose-
> colored, beyond which, in a murmur of silk, in panting
> whispers, the apotheosis of his youth assumed a thousand
> avatars.

> Between them low, far lights hung in the cool empty
> darkness blowing with fireflies.

The opposition is not Nature versus Machine or Popeye versus
Nature. Beauty can emerge anywhere, and it doesn't matter. A man
is executed unjustly for a crime he did not commit and it is followed
by a display of blooming in nature. The man guilty of that crime is

executed for another crime *he* did not commit and the blooming in nature follows just the same. The city, home of the Machine, can be a wonderland. The wilderness, home of Nature, can be a nightmare.

The imagery of the book supports these conclusions. Nature images are used to depict humans: the baseball game is "marsh-fowl disturbed by an alligator, not certain of where the danger is, motionless, poised, encouraging one another with short meaningless cries, plaintive, wary and forlorn." The coeds Horace meets in the station are like "identical artificial flowers surrounded each by bright and restless bees," and later "like honey poured in sunlight, pagan and evanescent and serene, thinly evocative of all lost days and outpaced delights, in the sun." As the book closes in the Luxembourg Gardens where Temple sits in triumphant ambiguity, the description combines nature images applied to the human scene with direct description of Nature robbed of its natural qualities.

> It had been a gray day, a gray summer, a gray year. . . .
> From beyond the circle with its spurious Greek balustrade,
> clotted with movement, filled with a gray light of the same
> color and texture as the water which the fountain played
> into the pool, came a steady crash of music. . . . In the
> pavilion a band in the horizon blue of the army played . . .
> while the twilight dissolved in wet gleams from the
> branches, onto the pavilion and the sombre toadstools of
> umbrellas. Rich and resonant the brasses crashed and died
> in the thick green twilight, rolling over them in rich sad
> waves. . . . Beside her her father sat . . . the rigid bar of
> his moustache beaded with moisture like frosted silver.
> She closed the compact and from beneath her smart new
> hat she seemed to follow with her eyes the waves of music,
> to dissolve into the dying brasses, across the pool and the
> opposite semicircle of trees where at sombre intervals the
> dead tranquil queens in stained marble mused, and on into
> the sky lying prone and vanquished in the embrace of the
> season of rain and death.

The ambiguity, the failure of nature and surroundings to govern anything in the slightest, and Temple's return to her beginning in indifference are all complete. Neutrality passes into self-dramatization and back to neutrality again. Temple's volitionless movement through the book is the source of the waves of accidence which destroy people, but she enters as an accident-prone innocent, proceeds into the maelstrom, and emerges at the end with some of that innocence (or at least a neutrality similar to that of Nature) intact.

When Popeye spits twice into the spring an expectation is aroused, and when he is terrified by the woods and the owl the expectation is strengthened. But like most of the expectations in the book, it is introduced just so that it can be overturned. We expect that the comfortable town, as safe as Aunt Jenny's distance from humanity, with its garden and October blooms and rose-colored shades, will provide the proper antidote for the poison of the enclave at Frenchman's Bend. But it turns out to have a poison of its own, more deadly because it disguises arbitrary accidence with certainty, establishment, and calm. When it is a comfy old sofa that conceals the remorseless fang, what greater terror can Popeye's grotesquerie conceal? The conventional order of things, society as refuge, community as rescuer, is overturned because the conventional order of things is in collaboration with nature: it takes poses and does nothing. Our expectations are as sure as our confidence that the cavalry, pennons flapping and bugles calling, must pour over the crest of the hill. Horace is good at heart and is the only conscience-armed instrument of the society. We expect that, as in Perry Mason, five minutes before the end of the program, as Hamilton Berger's eyes widen and his jaw drops, the witness will break down under his steely cross-examination and confess all, clearing all those people (including the defendant) who have been busy looking guilty as sin throughout the trial.

But the cavalry does not come and the witness is the steely one. Horace is betrayed by his sister, a mainstay of the same conventional order. When she goes to the district attorney for personal reasons, to extricate herself and Horace from damaging involvement, the district attorney goes to the Jew Lawyer for personal reasons, to win the case and gain political advantage, and the Jew Lawyer goes to Temple (here the direction of all these movements becomes clear) for the same reason Popeye does, because she has something he needs. We know that the good people will triumph. Temple crouches in the gas station, and there are good people on the road and all around her: someone will notice and then the people will stop this rape or theft or corruption or white slavery. But all those good people passing in and out of the scene, as obedient as the chorus in a Verdi opera, are no more effectual than the blind old man at the farm, who can only be affected by what he puts into his mouth.

The pattern is the same in Nature. Inexorable accident wins out over that rather lovely presence as surely as it does over the enclaves. Isolated incidents and personal aims must win out over the society of massed mankind. Nature is always present and usually lovely. Society, cities, Popeye, machines, all tarnish and blight it—but *it doesn't matter* because Nature has no force even at its full strength, other than its power to distract. Accidental injustice is followed by celebratory blooming and accidental justice is followed by an equally celebratory blooming. The people go to church, the people wander in Memphis and Oxford, the people assemble and look at Tommy's corpse. The people are as immanent and ineffectual as Nature.

The impact of both Nature and the people is dependent for narrative force upon contrasts which arouse expectation and end in defied expectations and denied hopes. The characters are groping and accidental, and their groping arouses more ridicule than empathy. If Horace is the hero, then the hero must fail, like the hero of *Paradise Lost*. Even worse, he is so feckless, so impotent (Faulkner used him as an emblem of impotence in *Sartoris*), that he must continually seem less interesting than his adversaries.

But Popeye is an even clearer case in point. The introduction of Popeye's biography in chapter 31, so late in the game, is a fictional device with a twisted purpose. It is a hangover from the conventional novel, a device of characterization designed to further the plot. There, the character who has appeared innocent and holier-than-the-hero has his past set forth in such a way as to cue in all of our unresolved questions of plot. But Popeye has clearly been wicked all along, and here we get not just instances of past wickedness, but genetic and environmental excuses for his development, and finally an ameliorative intimacy and humor in death row.

The section must throw the reader completely. Popeye looks like an antihero—but not exactly. The device finally forbids even comparatively sophisticated expectations: if the owl and the woods won't strike him down, then at least he can survive and, like The Mummy or Dracula of the horror movies, live on to be wicked once again. The reader is right here to resent the complete overturn of his expectations, however arcane those expectations may be. But I think Faulkner knew what he was doing, too. In a world in which Popeye is king and overturn is the rule, the law of psychological and sociological development can hold no more precedence than the laws of Nature or of man. The section comes on like explanation or even denouement, but its effect is only to accentuate accident, as explanation becomes excuse and excuse dissolves in enigma. The joke is, in one sense, a novelist's joke on us: the veil is lifted and what is revealed is more puzzling than what we had before. In another sense it is a rendering of a cosmic joke: all of our systems for explaining evil away by finding human cause or tracing environmental development fail. Their failure is as sure as that of the heaven-tree, the redbud, the dogwood and trial by jury.

Manipulated effects and reversed sympathies are combined in such a way that in the end Faulkner, as he overturns expectation after expectation, deprives us of essential balance. We can no longer find a horizon of morality or satisfaction or empathy, as character after character fails to confront the evil. In the distance, rising over the heads of Hogarth's grotesques and poverty and cruelty, there is the hint of an ideal to steer by. A row of overturned expectations must lead to some steadfast cliché or the expectations will cease to seem overturned. The reader is in free fall. *Sanctuary* in its defiance of expectation, its ideal of reversal, its carefully calculated distance from human feeling, refuses to introduce a necessary isle of repose. Because of this it is more exciting in memory than while it is being read. Its characters stand in the memory and their myth is true at a distance. We believe in them because we believe in what we have been through in the experience of their events. But the book while we were reading it denied us empathy, denied us a place to stand, denied us all our essential comforts, and manipulated us so frantically that we could not believe it while it was happening.

Faulkner did not make the same mistake twice any more than he wrote the same book twice (even *Big Woods* is a different book made of old parts). *Light in August* has Lena and Byron, *Absalom* has Judith and even Quentin, and the later books are firmly in the control of *us* figures, firmly in the hands of men rather than gods. Trees act like trees and mobs are generally brought to their senses by an obliging *us*-surrogate. Only here is coldness uncompromised, objectivity heartless, the performance more important to Faulkner than the audience.

Sanctuary: From Confrontation to Peaceful Void

Calvin S. Brown

> . . . thinking Now what? What now? and answering himself: Why,
> nothing. Nothing. It's finished.
>
> Sanctuary

Sanctuary has been one of Faulkner's most consistently popular
novels with the general reader, and one of the most enigmatic to
literary criticism. Some critics recognize its enigmatic quality, but
most tend to be quite positive (Ambrose Bierce defined positive as
"mistaken at the top of one's voice") in their readings of it, and it is
only when we compare their dogmatic statements that the enigma
appears in its full flower. First of all, suppose we ask Faulknerian
critics how good or how bad a novel *Sanctuary* is. Though Hyatt
Waggoner has some reservations, he considers it "one of the finest
novels in modern literature," and Edmund Volpe agrees that it
"deserves to be ranked just behind Faulkner's greatest works."
Conrad Aiken finds that it "betrays a genius for form, quite apart
from its wonderful virtuosity in other respects." But George
Marion O'Donnell considers it to be "fundamentally a caricature";
and in spite of some good qualities, to Walter Slatoff it "remains to
a large extent a pot-boiler." Joachim Seyppel agrees, with a defense
that is almost more damning than utter condemnation: "The best
that can be said for this production is . . . that there are worse
pot-boilers."

From *Mosaic* 7, no. 1 (Fall 1973), special issue: *The Novels of William Faulkner,* edited
by R. G. Collins and Kenneth McRobbie. © 1973 by the Editors, *Mosaic.* University
of Manitoba Press, 1973.

If we ask what the novel is about, we get a bewildering variety of answers. Dr. Lawrence Kubie knows that it is about the fear of impotence. Irving Howe characteristically considers it an attack on "the modern South in particular and modern life in general," in the form of a "Manichean morality play." In a similar vein, Frederick J. Hoffman reads it as "one of Faulkner's most nearly exhaustive commentaries . . . upon modern society." Melvin Backman considers it a "sociological drama"—a phrase which might mean much the same thing as a Manichean morality play or something very different. Many other critics see *Sanctuary* as an attack on modern society, but Hyatt Waggoner dismisses this whole school of criticism with the flat statement that "in *Sanctuary* the element of social criticism and moral judgment does not come to much." If it is not about modern society, then what is it about? "It is surely one of the most telling reflections on the fall of New World man," says Lewis Simpson. But Peter Swiggart believes that "In *Sanctuary* Faulkner is mainly concerned with individual futility and despair." William Rossky considers the social and individual malaise, the modern dehumanization and mechanization, to be merely surface phenomena: they cannot be ignored, but "it is rather to a universal cosmic terror that the nightmare of *Sanctuary* is most essentially related."

What is the importance of *Sanctuary* in Faulkner's development? We get diametrically opposite answers to this question. Mario Materassi tells us that "in *Sanctuary* the writer finds himself: the point of view is now that of a harsh, if not downright ferocious, critic of the surrounding society" (my translation). But Joachim Seyppel thinks not: "Faulkner had already outgrown *Sanctuary* before he finished it" (my translation).

George Marion O'Donnell interpreted the novel as an elaborate and detailed allegory, but Malcolm Cowley contradicted him with the flat statement that "*Sanctuary* is not a connected allegory."

As for the comic episodes, William Van O'Connor accused Faulkner of "sometimes introducing scenes that in the main are irrelevant, like the affairs of Fonzo and Virgil Snopes or the beer guzzling of Uncle Bud," and Irving Howe likewise found the comic chapters "not essential to the theme of the novel," though he considered them "the finest in the book." But several critics, most importantly Cleanth Brooks, have been at some pains to demonstrate that "the comic scenes are not . . . extraneous to the novel."

Finally, we may ask about the nature of the characters in

Sanctuary—Popeye, for example. To many critics he is and remains an enigma, but to others he is quite obvious. He is "the symbol of mechanical civilization" to Earl Miner, but Robert Slabey is convinced that he is Hermes. Elmo Howell considers that "Popeye is an allegorical figure . . . the abstract of evil." But Faulkner himself (speaking some thirty years after the writing of *Sanctuary* and hence not making a really hippostomatic statement) rejected this sort of interpretation: "No, he was to me another lost human being" (Gwynn and Blotner, eds.).

In the face of such a welter of conflicting opinions, it would be absurd to produce another reading of *Sanctuary* with the hope of solving all problems or convincing all readers. The comments which follow are made with the primary intention of pointing out a fundamental structural pattern of *Sanctuary* which has not been noted before, and the secondary hope of convincing some readers and interesting the rest.

My basic point is that *Sanctuary* begins with a series of personal confrontations between constantly shifting pairs of strongly contrasted characters whose different backgrounds and personalities are kept before the reader by their highly individualized styles of speech. From these personal encounters it moves on to a primarily comic series of confrontations between groups, concepts, or attitudes of one sort or another. Finally, the confrontations do not lead to resolutions: they simply fade out, leaving only apathy and indifference, an acceptance of the essential meaninglessness of the cosmos which constitutes the final attitude of the characters and the final position of the novel itself.

In the famous opening scene of *Sanctuary,* Popeye and Horace Benbow confront each other across a spring for more than two hours, with only a couple of brief conversations, and then go on together to the Old Frenchman Place. The two men are opposites in almost all respects. Horace is "a tall, thin man"; Popeye is "a man of under size." Horace is hatless; Popeye has a slanted straw hat. Horace carries his coat; Popeye wears his. Horace has a book in his pocket; Popeye has a pistol. Horace knows the book-name of a bird he hears, and finally manages to remember the local name too; Popeye is terrified when an owl swoops by. Horace drinks from the spring; Popeye spits into it. And so the contrasts continue.

One of the most striking of these contrasts is the two languages spoken. Later in the novel we get to expect Horace to talk in a bookish, abstract, rhetorical, pseudo-poetical vein. (Horace is a thoroughly academic type, and consequently critics, being also academic types, have a good deal of trouble seeing him for what he is. They tend to give him the benefit of a doubt even when there is none, calling his blatant artiness artistic sensitivity, for example.) At the spring, though, Horace is not in a rhetorical vein, but in a confessional one. Under the pretext of identifying himself, he begins to babble about his affairs, in short sentences dominated by the pronoun *I*: "I'm a lawyer in Kinston. I used to live in Jefferson yonder; I'm on my way there now." He uses eight first-person pronouns in seven lines. And when he later becomes bookish and ornate in his speech, he does nothing to change the impression of self-centeredness.

Popeye's language is totally different.

> "You can't stop me like this," Benbow said. "Suppose I break and run."
> Popeye put his eyes on Benbow, like rubber. "Do you want to run?"
> "No," Benbow said.
> Popeye removed his eyes. "Well, dont, then."

This is his usual laconic style throughout the whole book. He rarely makes statements. Usually, as here, he talks in a mixture of questions and orders. The questions are seldom used to elicit information; they are implied threats, and the orders are their logical conclusion.

> "What're you doing here?" Popeye said.
> "Aint doin nothing," Tommy said.
> "Are you following me around?"
> "I aint trailin nobody," Tommy said sullenly.
> "Well, dont, then," Popeye said.

> "Stop it, now. You going to shut it?"
> "Yes," she whimpered.
> "See you do, then. Come on. Get yourself fixed."

The vocabularies of Popeye and Horace are as sharply differentiated as the general patterns of their speech. Popeye uses a number of words and phrases of urban slang which are foreign to the world of Yoknapatawpha County and seldom or never occur elsewhere in Faulkner. These expressions—"Go take a pill"; "ginneys"; "Buy yourself a hoop"; "Keep [the change]. You'll get rich faster"—all have a smarty-contemptuous ring. The most conspicuous one is *Jack* as an all-purpose name applied to almost any male, from Horace at the beginning of the book to the Alabama sheriff who springs the trap on Popeye at the end. Popeye also uses the urban and cosmo-politan *Jesus Christ!* as an expression of frustration or dissatisfaction, where the indigenous Yoknapatawpha equivalent would be *God damn!*

Horace Benbow uses neither of these, preferring the literary *damnation*. When he really gets into his bookish vein his speech becomes ludicrously inappropriate to his surroundings and his audience—because he is really talking to, for, and about himself. At the Old Frenchman Place he harangues the wild assortment of urban gangsters, cosmopolitian moonshiners, and local rustics about the "reaffirmation of the old ferment," "the green-snared promise of unease," and "the slain flowers, and delicate dead flowers and tears." No wonder Ruby Lamar, listening to him thinks "He's crazy," and "The fool, . . . the poor fool."

Ruby Lamar and Temple Drake form another sharply contrasted pair, in speech as in everything else. We know little about Ruby except that her faithful following of Goodwin has given her consid-erable periods of residence in San Francisco, New York, and Leavenworth. She comes from a lower-class family (presumably in the South), but she and Lee have moved here and there. The status and customs of her family are made plain by her account of her father's shooting her lover. It is incredible that several critics who profess to speak authoritatively on Southern society have made the blunder of attributing this episode to the Drake family and the account of it to Temple. Even if Faulkner were not perfectly specific on this point, the language of the family is a clear enough indication. Temple's youngest brother, at the time of *Sanctuary,* might well have threatened to protect or to avenge his sister's honor, but he would certainly not have "said he would kill the goddam son of a bitch."

As the most admirable person in the novel, Ruby serves as something of a moral norm. This function is reinforced by her speech, which is also something of a norm. It is a standard colloquial English, without any specifically local features. The sentences are short, concise, forceful. The vocabulary is timeless, or as nearly so as a vocabulary can be. Faulkner achieves this effect by a judicious combination of contemporary slang and ancient archaic expressions. Ruby says that she cooks "for crimps and spungs and feebs," and she tells Temple that, after getting Goodwin out of Leavenworth, "then I could quit jazzing" (fornicating). But there is a fine Elizabethan ring to her language when she calls Temple a "little doll-faced slut" and when she reports that her father, having shot her lover down, told her, "Get down there and sup your dirt, you whore."

Temple is Ruby's opposite in all respects. She comes of an upper-class family that, in her at least, has gone to bad seed. She is "long legged, thin armed, with high, small buttocks—a small childish figure no longer quite a child, not yet quite a woman"; but Ruby's "breast moved deep and full." Faulkner keeps this contrast before us by regularly calling Temple by name, but referring to Ruby simply as "the woman"; and when Ruby inadvertently called Temple a woman, she immediately corrected herself. When Horace was trying to find out what had happened at the Old Frenchman Place, " 'There was a woman there,' she said. 'A young girl.' " Temple's perpetual histrionics contrast strongly with Ruby's realistic stoicism. Temple is always watching herself and calculating her effect on others. She is fond of astonished reflections on her dramatic plight—an infantile attitude shared, appropriately, by Gowan Stevens. Even her actions are calculatedly dramatic. We are constantly told that she ran, spun, sprang, whirled, snatched, flung, and so on. Faulkner tells us that on one occasion, Temple "laid her hand on the cold stove." A moment later she "saw her hand lying on the stove. She snatched it up with a wailing shriek, clapping it against her mouth, and turned and ran toward the door." Ruby would not have made this sort of commotion even if the stove had actually been hot. She never puts on a show. She simply does the best she can and bears whatever must be borne.

Temple's language is like Ruby's in that it is not particularly localized. But it is clearly particularized as the self-consciously childish slangy cuteness of a flapper of the late twenties: "and Daddy would just die" (if he found out); "Be a sport"; "You mean old thing!" Temple talks baby-talk ostentatiously to Ruby's baby—a thing which Ruby herself never does. Her narrative is strung together childishly with *and* after *and*. There is one amusing instance of the difference of language as well as attitude in parallel situations. Temple tells Ruby, "Buddy—that's Hubert, my youngest brother—said that if he ever caught me with a drunk man, he'd beat hell out of me." When Ruby cites the parallel in her own life, where they play for keeps instead of "playing at it"—as she correctly accuses Temple of doing—she paraphrases the flip "beat hell out of me" into standard English, and follows it with the violent idiom of people who are not playing at it. "My brother said he would kill Frank. He didn't say he would give me a whipping if he caught me with him; he said he would kill the goddam son of a bitch."

All these differences of background, attitude, and idiom come to a focus in the big confrontation between Ruby and Temple, where Ruby tells Temple off for her childish and gutless histrionics based on a social situation which protects her from the natural consequences of her acts and attitudes, and lets her get by with being a selfish tease.

It is possible to pair off other characters in *Sanctuary,* much as Popeye can be paired with Horace, and Temple with Ruby. We have, for example, Narcissa and Miss Jenny, similar in general background, but utterly different in age, character, and intelligence. But the pairings are, in any case, only temporary. Though we have the clear playing off of Popeye against Horace and of Temple against Ruby early in the book, later on the contrasting pairs thrown into close relationship are Horace and Ruby, on the one hand, and Temple and Popeye, on the other. The technique of *Sanctuary* does not lie, then, in setting up pairs of permanently contrasted characters, but in setting up a series of shifting and temporary oppositions. For this purpose Faulkner requires a gallery of people with widely different backgrounds and characters, and with characteristic modes of speech which keep their differences always in evidence. In addition to the characters already mentioned, for example, we have Tommy, a pure local rustic who has been to Jefferson only "on infrequent Saturdays," and has probably never been further from Frenchman's Bend than Jefferson. His rusticity is exaggerated by his weakness of mind, and he speaks and thinks primarily in fixed rural Yoknapatawpha expressions—"I be dawg if he aint a case, now"; "Durn them fellers." His ineffectual benevolence gives a special poignancy to his rusticity and feeblemindedness. (Is it going too far to see Tommy's ineffectual goodness of heart as a sort of parody of the same quality in Horace, just as we can see Fonzo and Virgil's initiation into evil as a parody of Temple's?)

Other conspicuously individualized characters include State Senator Clarence Snopes, with his air of bluff, friendly heartiness vainly trying to conceal his rapacious chicanery, just as the pomposity of his language vainly tries to conceal his illiteracy. And then there is the hard-boiled, good-hearted sentimentalist Miss Reba, with her somewhat cosmopolitan sub-standard speech (*nuttin,* for example, where the Yoknapatawpha equivalent would be *nothin*) always tottering on the verge of the whorehouse vernacular and often falling into it.

Faulkner brings these varied characters into a constantly shifting series of pairings, so that the basic structure of the novel can best be described as a series of confrontations. The opening one, between Popeye and Horace Benbow, sets the tone. When the pair reach the Old Frenchman Place, Popeye tells Ruby to cook for Horace too, and a confrontation between Popeye and Ruby develops, beginning with Ruby's hostile "Why tell me?" and ending with her repeated exclamation, "You bastard." And so the narrative proceeds. At the supper which follows, the group eats "silently and steadily"; general conversation has no place in the world of *Sanctuary,* where practically every conversation begins as a confrontation or develops into one. After supper, when Horace harangues the group on the porch about himself, he immediately goes into a long account—quoting all the dialogue—of a confrontation between himself and Little Belle about a boy she had picked up on a train. As the evening progresses we have a set of mounting confrontations between Goodwin and Ruby, culminating in his holding her hands and giving her a good slapping, and a similar set between Van and Gowan—the petty hoodlum and the fake gentleman—culminating eventually in knockouts for both of them. There is a similar mounting series involving Popeye and Tommy over the issue of following around. First of all, Tommy tells, with simpleminded amusement, how Popeye shot Tommy's dog for sniffing at his heels. Then, in a passage already quoted, Popeye warns Tommy not to follow him. Finally, in the barn, the same formula of question and command build up to its climax.

> Popeye laid his hand flat on Tommy's face and thrust him back and leaned past him and looked up at the house. Then he looked at Tommy.
> "Didn't I tell you about following me?"
> "I wasn't following you," Tommy said. "I was watching him," jerking his head toward the house.
> "Watch him, then," Popeye said. Tommy turned his head and looked toward the house.

Then Popeye shot him in the back of the head.

It is worth some time to show how largely confrontations dominate all the earlier part of *Sanctuary.* Other major ones include those between Horace and his sister Narcissa over his involvement with the Goodwin case, those between Horace and Clarence Snopes (marked by craft and superficial friendship rather than open hostility) over Clarence's information about Temple, those between Popeye and Temple on the way to Memphis, those between Miss Reba and Temple about Temple's seeing the doctor and her seeing Horace, and a number of others. Sometimes the possibilities of confrontation are systematically exhausted. When Temple tries to get Popeye to drive her and Gowan to town, the first one ends when Popeye says to Gowan, "Make your whore lay off me, Jack." Gowan then turns on Popeye with vague verbal aggression and threat, only to be met with silent contempt. Then Temple abuses Popeye a bit, and ends by taunting Gowan for discreetly making her stop. There are three possible combinations of three persons taken two at a time, and Faulkner has systematically gone through the three possibilities. The same thing is done later with Temple, Popeye, and Red in the roadhouse before Red's murder.

Minor confrontations are everywhere. When Gowan spends the night carousing with the town boys in Jefferson, he and Doc take an instant dislike to each other, and it is only the pacifying efforts of the other boys, who serve as a sort of background for the intermittent confrontation, that avert physical hostilities. When Temple thinks of the girls in the dormitory dressing for a dance, she recalls a confrontation between a group of virgins and a nonvirgin with her eyes "courageous and frightened and daring" surrounded by the virgins with "their eyes like knives until you could almost watch her flesh where the eyes were touching it."

Many other brief scenes of minor confrontation are recalled or described, but even more significant are the minimal encounters which serve only to create the feeling that life, as here depicted, is essentially a series of hostile pairings. When Horace and Tommy get to Popeye's liquor truck, a couple of unidentified hangers-on of Popeye are there.

> "You took your time," one of the men said. "Didn't you? I aimed to be halfway to town by now. I got a woman waiting for me."
> "Sure," the other man said. "Waiting on her back." The first man cursed him.

As Temple lay in bed at Miss Reba's listening to the sounds from the street, "once two voices quarreling bitterly came up and beneath the shade." The confrontation of unknowns may be ambivalent.

> In an alley-mouth two figures stood, face to face, not touching; the man speaking in a low tone unprintable epithet after epithet in a caressing whisper, the woman motionless before him as though in a musing swoon of voluptuous ecstasy.

Minimal confrontations flare even between boy and beast, when Uncle Bud tries to keep Miss Reba's dogs from chewing up her shoes.

> "Scat!" the boy said, striking at one of them with his hand. The dog's head snapped around, its teeth clicking, its half-hidden eyes bright and malevolent. The boy recoiled. "You bite me, you thon bitch," he said.

In fact, in the atmosphere of *Sanctuary,* hostile encounters are so much the norm that those of animals are suggested by inanimate sounds. When Clarence Snopes telephoned Horace from a cafe, there was a background of music.

> Against Horace's ear the radio or the victrola performed a reedy arpeggio of saxophones. Obscene, facile, they seemed to be quarreling with one another, like two dexterous monkeys in a cage.

Once we are even left in doubt as to whether the enemy is man or beast, or perhaps asthma or the universe itself: "Beyond the wall Miss Reba filled the hall, the house, with a harsh choking uproar of obscene cursing."

In the first half of *Sanctuary,* then, the primary technique is to create a set of characters who have little in common, and to bring them together at close quarters and let them at each other's throats. A moonshiner's hangout is the perfect setting for the purpose, since it must have its local staff and its contacts with the bootleggers who distribute its product. It is also a place where a college playboy may take his illicit date to replenish his supply. But Temple is not really there against her will. It is true that Popeye has given orders for Temple and Gowan to be brought to the house, but it is Temple who insists on going into the house, to the extent of not even answering when Gowan asks why she doesn't wait outside. Of all the people that appear at Lee Goodwin's, only Horace, who had stopped at the spring for a drink and been brought to the house by Popeye on suspicion, is there against his will, and Horace is not there at the time of the crucial events. The rest are a motley crowd of incompatible people brought together by discreditable motives and ready to fly out at each other for any or no reason. All but Ruby, Popeye, and Temple have Lee's moonshine as an extra spur to belligerence. (There is so little to be said for Temple in general that it should be noted to her credit that she does not drink at the Old Frenchman Place. Like any other flapper, she had doubtless had a few surreptitious drinks on dates, but her serious drinking begins at Miss Reba's and then develops with horrifying speed).

But we cannot conclude that liquor or crime is the real cause of the contentiousness. They simply make the Old Frenchman Place a particularly fine spot for observing the general rancor which flourishes equally in Horace's serene and stupid sister Narcissa and in the hotel clerk and in the preacher and the ladies of the Baptist church.

With the Baptists we come to the possibility of confrontations of groups and social institutions. These are never developed in the obvious form. The Baptists seem to have persecuted Ruby more as a loose confederation of kindred spirits than as an actual organization, but the idea of a confrontation between their principles and their practice is inherent in the situation. It is implied when Miss Jenny dismisses their conduct, apparently as normal, predictable, and trivial, with the deprecatory remark that "They're just Baptists," and it is bitterly emphasized in Horace's sarcastic "Christians. Christians."

Faulkner's real development of social confrontations takes a different tack. He presents it as a wild comedy of incongruities. The burlesque episodes of Fonzo and Virgil at Miss Reba's (a wild variation on She Stoops to Conquer), Red's funeral, and Miss Reba's tea party after the funeral have often been taken as modern forms of the frontiersman's tall tale, and in a sense this is what they are. But they go beyond their models in that they are concerned with incongruities a good deal more fundamental than that between sober fact and the natural human tendency to exaggerate. Actually, they have a good deal more in common with the tall tales of Gulliver's Travels than with yarns like "The Big Bear of Arkansas." Like Swift, Faulkner presents us with scenes which are amusing in themselves and are obviously exaggerations of normal experiences, but the essence of the matter lies not so much in the exaggerations as in the normal experiences on which they make an indirect commentary. And the commentary works primarily by means of a logical combination of things which are—or at first glance seem to be—essentially incongruent.

The episode of Fonzo and Virgil at Miss Reba's comes first, and prepares the way for the others. It is the closest of all the burlesque episodes to pure humor, as opposed to satire, because the incongruity here is more apparent than real. The idea of two naive country boys living in a brothel under the impression that it is a rooming house is amusing enough, but the alacrity and delight with which these boys learn about whorehouses shows that no moral incongruity is involved, but only a physical misunderstanding. On their twelfth night in Memphis, the boys visit a brothel, and from this time on they would presumably be delighted to learn what Miss Reba's house really is. As they learn more both about Miss Reba's and about other whorehouses, they are sure to find out, rather sooner than later, where they are living. But Faulkner diverts our attention with Clarence Snopes and the Negro brothel, so that he can leave them in ignorance as to their boardinghouse. This is a wise solution of a difficult problem, for the moment of truth could hardly be anything more than an anticlimax.

This episode is such pure, lighthearted comedy that it disarms all but the most dogged searchers for social significance. It is interesting to compare it with the episode in Thomas Mann's *Doktor Faustus* in which Adrian Leverkühn similarly finds himself, by misapprehension, in a brothel. Adrian's experience is symbolic and ultimately tragic, and it determines the course of his life and of his art as a composer. But with Fonzo and Virgil, Faulkner is content to stay, for the moment, on the amusing surface of things without probing for their significance or consequences. The probings are reserved for the comedies of incongruity which are to follow.

One of the very few things on which critics of *Sanctuary* are in general agreement is the fact that the account of Red's funeral is a brilliant performance. But that is as far as the agreement goes. Should we join with Campbell and Foster in enjoying it as "an example of surrealistic humor," or should we shudder with Irving Howe, who finds it to be "a kind of expressionist nightmare?" Once we go beyond the obvious fact that the scene presents a brilliant use of incongruity, almost any approach is possible, and most have been taken by one critic or another. But there is one element in the presentation that seems not to have been remarked, and that is the double-edged satire. Everyone sees that the roadhouse funeral of Red is a sort of parody or burlesque of our sanctimoniously materialistic mortuary folkways. But we do not come from church to the roadhouse, and thus get a contrast; in the novel there is no interval between the extended account of the normal operation of the joint on the evening when Red was murdered and the description of his funeral. When we last see Red alive, he is standing at the crap table. Two pages later, his funeral flowers are on it. The result is that the holding of the funeral in the roadhouse gives us an incongruity without a norm, and the setting does not clash with the occasion any more than the occasion clashes with the setting. If the roadhouse makes a mockery of the funeral, the funeral likewise makes a mockery of the roadhouse. The roadhouse equivalents of the normal music, sermon, and mourners are neither more nor less absurd than the funerary uses of the dance floor and crap table. If we sympathize with the proprietor who—appropriately—wants to observe the proprieties, we must sympathize equally with the woman in red who, as an old habitué of the place, resents having the body in the way and shouts "Get that damn stiff out of here and open up the game."

Faulkner sets up the incongruities in his own introduction to the funeral scene. He begins with a straight, factual account of the arrangements, but soon remarks sardonically that the flowers were "in wreaths and crosses and other shapes of ceremonial mortality." The waiters moved about "with swaggering and decorous repression," and the scene had "a hushed, macabre air a little febrile." The mixture of funeral and bright new spring clothes increased "the atmosphere of macabre paradox" and from this point on the scene can be left to build up from paradox to confrontation and on to violence. What happens here seems very much like the earlier build-up of hostilities between Gowan and Van, except that this time the confrontation is between groups. But there is an important difference. The encounters between Gowan and Van were merely personal, but the groups that fight around Red's coffin and finally overturn it represent different institutions, different values, different goals. It is a battle of church against roadhouse, stuffy decorum against hectic hedonism, human dignity against human desires. And since the balance has been carefully maintained and each group has been allowed to undercut the other, the reader is not involved on either side and can watch the whole performance with disinterested amusement. Presumably when the corpse "tumbled slowly and sedately out," everyone quieted down, for after this there are no longer fighting factions, but only a unified and anonymous "they" who combined their efforts to raise the corpse and repair it as best they could. What happens here is exactly like the sudden calm after the fight between Gowan and Van turns into a free-for-all at the Old Frenchman Place, even to the identical act of cooperating to pick up an inert body:

> Then it was over, gone like a furious gust of black wind, leaving a peaceful vacuum in which they moved quietly about, lifting Gowan out of the weeds with low-spoken, amicable directions to one another.

Everything has cancelled out, and the factions have forgotten their differences. Neither side has won, or, more accurately, both sides have won: decorum has been reestablished—but the damn stiff is being got out of there.

In the entire account of Red's funeral there is not one single identifiable character that appears anywhere else in the novel. All the roles are walk-on parts. In the nature of things most of the participants would have to be strangers, but it is plain that Faulkner used this fact to insure the reader's impartiality and detachment. Miss Reba is the proof. We know that she went to the funeral, but we do not see her there, nor do we know how she reacted to the wild goings-on and the drunken brawl, for in the scene that follows she and her two colleagues are so resolutely decorous that there is no hint of these matters, and the references to the funeral are simply the social small change on grief and mortality that follows any conventional funeral.

Her tea party with her two colleagues and the bibulous child called Uncle Bud is a comic masterpiece. Conrad Aiken comments that the scene "is quite false, taken out of its context; it is not endowed with the same *kind* of actuality which permeates the greater part of the book at all." I am not sure that it is as unreal as Aiken implies. Perhaps it is the actuality of Miss Reba's house that is of a different kind from the actuality of the Jefferson jail or the Old Frenchman Place or the parlor at Sartoris. Be that as it may, the actuality of this scene is of exactly the same kind as that of Fonzo and Virgil and of Red's obsequies. Once again we have a confrontation of attitudes and social institutions, but this time there are no conflicting groups and no violence. There is simply the incongruity between the basic reality of brothel life and manners and the thin veneer of pseudo-elegant decorum with which it is covered—a veneer that is constantly cracking and peeling so that the whorehouse underneath shows through more and more clearly as the scene progresses. The satire here is no longer Swiftian, but is more in the vein of *Le Bourgeois Gentilhomme* and *The Beggar's Opera*.

Once again Faulkner sets the stage by his own comments at the beginning. After Miss Reba has begun the party by taking off her shoes and the other two have pretended to be shocked at Uncle Bud's infantile effort to call the snapping dog a son of a bitch, they return to the conventional funereal platitudes, and Faulkner firmly sets the tone of fake elegance.

> They drank, bowing formally to one another. The fat woman dried her eyes; the two guests wiped their lips with prim decorum. The thin one coughed delicately aside, behind her hand. . . . They began to talk politely, in decorous half-completed sentences, with little gasps of agreement.

This time, however, Faulkner does not simply turn the scene over to the events and characters. Much of the comedy is linguistic, as in Miss Myrtle's "reely" for *really*—her everyday pronunciation is probably "rilly." Or in the clash between the formal diction and the vulgar endearment when she replies to a question of Miss Lorraine with "I wouldn't undertake to say, dearie." As they drink more and more (and progress from beer to gin) the veneer begins to disintegrate, and when they decide to send Uncle Bud out so that Miss Reba can tell them freely about Popeye's sexual aberrations, it almost disappears, but not quite. Faulkner has kept the attempts at elegant manners before us by his description, and they continue to clash with the increasingly vulgar language and its indecent content. Miss Myrtle's repetitive affectations about "us poor girls" and Miss Reba's moral outrage at Popeye's perversion add to the incongruities. Near the end of the scene these elements all combine at close quarters. Miss Reba is speaking.

"If you want to turn a stud in to your girl" I says "go somewhere else to do it. I aint going to have my house turned into no French joint."

"The son of a bitch," Miss Lorraine said.

"He'd ought to've had sense enough to got a old ugly man," Miss Myrtle said. "Tempting us poor girls like that."

"Men always expects us to resist temptation," Miss Lorraine said. She was sitting upright like a schoolteacher. "The lousy son of a bitch."

Once again, after a bit more in the same vein, when the comedy has gone far enough, Faulkner rings down the curtain with an outrageous deus ex machina. With Virgil and Fonzo it had been Clarence and his Negro brothel. With Red's funeral it had been the dumping of the corpse. This time it is the drunken vomiting of Uncle Bud.

Goodwin's trial continues many of the themes and devices of the comic scenes, but on a totally different level. Any trial is, by definition, a confrontation: that is the essence of the adversary system of jurisprudence. But the real confrontation is not between Horace Benbow and the district attorney. Though we are given a few moments of the actual trial, it is plain that Horace does not put up enough resistance to make the trial any sort of real confrontation. In spite of his assurances to the Goodwins, he seems to have accepted defeat long before it comes. In fact, he seems almost to look forward to it. Perhaps he is a good lawyer for documents and estates, but unused to criminal practice, or perhaps he is merely incredibly naive. At any rate, it is hopelessly unrealistic to think that a case is won because the opposition is "reduced to trying to impugn the character of your witness," instead of countering the attempt. Horace puzzles the judge by repeatedly failing to make legitimate objections to the prosecutor's flagrant prejudicial procedures, objections which the judge is prepared to sustain. It is true that Temple's perjury is a severe blow to Horace's case and that possibly no lawyer could have won in the face of such odds; but it is also true that Horace had given up before the perjury occurred and would probably have lost his case even without it.

Much has been written about the reasons for Temple's perjury. Peter Lisca invented the theory that her father the judge and her brothers made her perjure herself to save her and their reputations, and though Cleanth Brooks completely demolished this theory, it still has adherents ("Some New Light on Faulkner's *Sanctuary*"). Only one point in this controversy seems worth noting here. Lisca cites Temple's "parrotlike answers" on the stand as evidence that she was repeating memorized testimony, and hence was perjuring herself on someone else's orders. But, earlier, Temple had "added a phrase, glibly obscene, with a detached parrotlike effect" and had murmured to Red "in parrotlike underworld epithet." Parrotlike utterances are evidently characteristic of Temple long before her family knows of her involvement with the underworld. Further-more, drilling witnesses on the wording of their replies is a common enough legal practice. Horace had spent a good deal of the previous night in the jail drilling Ruby. We do not see her answering questions on the stand, but her answers were presumably as parrotlike as Temple's. At any rate, they should have been. When Horace finished a drilling session lasting well over three hours, he told Ruby:

> I think that's all. Can you remember it, now? If he should ask you anything you cant answer in the exact words you've learned tonight, just say nothing for a moment. I'll attend to the rest. Can you remember, now?

If parrotlike answers are evidence of suborned perjury, then Horace and Ruby must stand convicted too.

Fear of Popeye, or willingness to go along with him in this matter at least, might well have caused Temple's perjury, and Brooks makes a good case for this explanation. Another interesting theory derives the main significance of Temple's act from Faulkner's omission of any overt reason. After considering various possible explanations, Heinrich Straumann concludes that

> the mere fact that Faulkner provides no direct explanation for Temple's conduct can actually mean only that evil, as such, is supposed to be plainly the determining element. In this case the narrative omission would function as a moral indication. (My translation.)

There is, however, another highly plausible motive which seems to have been ignored. Not only were Temple and Ruby opposites in many respects, but they seem to have developed an immediate antipathy to each other. Even the difference between the scrawny girl and the full-breasted woman seems to have played its part, as is hinted in Temple's account of imagining herself as a forty-five-year-old schoolteacher "all big up here like women get," and in Ruby's reference to New York during the war, with "even the ratty little girls wearing silk." At the Old Frenchman Place the antipathy came into the open in the big confrontation when Ruby mercilessly exposed Temple for the little gutless doll-faced playing-at-it slut that she was, and thereby reduced her to a crushed and almost pitiable creature. This scene had blown over, superficially, as violent scenes in *Sanctuary* so often do. It had ended with Ruby urging Temple to go on and eat her supper, and later Ruby had taken Temple under her protecting wing for the night. But even while doing so, Ruby had "turned and jerked Temple up to her, and gripping her by the shoulders, their faces close together, she cursed Temple in a whisper, a sound no louder than a sigh and filled with fury." Evidently there had been no abatement of hostilities, nor was there any during the night that Temple and Ruby spent together in the crib.

When Temple was finally driving away from the Old French-man Place in Popeye's car, Ruby met them as she was walking from the spring back to the house. Here is the meeting, seen from Ruby's point of view.

> Popeye did not make any sign, though Temple looked full at the woman. From beneath her hat Temple looked the woman full in the face, without any sign of recognition whatsoever. The face did not turn, the eyes did not wake; to the woman beside the road it was like a small, dead-colored mask drawn past her on a string and then away.

And here is the encounter as Temple saw it.

> Before they came to the tree they passed the woman. She stood beside the road, carrying the child, the hem of her dress folded back over its face, and she looked at them quietly from beneath the faded sunbonnet, flicking swiftly in and out of Temple's vision without any motion, any sign.

When Miss Reba is trying to persuade Temple to talk to Horace, she makes an appeal for the sake of Ruby and the child as well as Goodwin.

"They're going to hang him for something he never done," Miss Reba said. "And she wont have nuttin, nobody. And you with diamonds, and her with that poor little kid. You seen it, didn't you?"

Does Miss Reba inadvertently suggest to Temple a way to pay Ruby out for her own humiliation? It seems very probable that she does. At any rate, the first time that the two women meet after passing on the road, Temple takes the stand and pins the murder on Ruby's man, and the last time we see Ruby she is in the exact situation predicted by Miss Reba.

Perhaps it is pointless to assume that Temple perjured herself for any one clear reason, and the question should be couched in terms of her several reasons and their relative influence on the final act. I am convinced, however, that reprisal against Ruby is one of the strongest reasons, if not the only one.

In any case, the central confrontation in the trial, that between law and justice, does not depend on this single act of one person. Justice is thwarted not only by Temple's deliberate lying, but by the district attorney's successful attempts to prejudice the jury by irrelevant questions and overheated, hypocritical rhetoric, by the judge's role which requires him to let these tactics get by to a considerable extent as long as Horace does not object, and by the connivance of people like Narcissa Benbow and Clarence Snopes. But here there is no standoff or reconciliation between the opposing forces; the triumph of injustice is complete and final. There is an ironical twist in that the possible forms of this injustice have been seen all along as death by hanging, at the state's hands, or death by a bullet from Popeye or his henchmen. No one has been concerned about the possibility of lynching; but the lawlessness of the mob merely anticipates the injustice already decreed by the law.

So far, we have seen *Sanctuary* as proceeding from a series of personal confrontations to a series of group, institutional, or abstract ones. The division is somewhat blurred by the facts that the group confrontations begin well before they come to dominate, and that the individual ones do not entirely stop when the group ones begin, but it is nevertheless a very real change in the texture of the novel. The third and final stage has a similarly blurred line of demarcation, but is equally real. It is a stage of withdrawal, apathy, indifference. Not only does Horace seem to give up before Temple makes his case hopeless, Goodwin does the same thing while the trial is still in progress. He has been cowering in a corner of his cell out of range of the narrow window through which he thinks Popeye will shoot him. But the night before the last day of the trial, he sits with "his legs extended in the attitude of a man in the last stage of physical exhaustion," directly in front of it. The next morning Horace offered to arrange for Goodwin to stay in his cell and not go to court, but Goodwin expected to be shot on the way there, and apparently welcomed the opportunity:

> "No," Goodwin said. "I'm sick of it. I'm going to get
> it over with. Just tell that goddamned deputy not to walk
> too close to me."

This is the mood and tone of the final section of *Sanctuary*. The free-for-all at the Old Frenchman Place, suddenly blowing over and quickly forgotten, offers a sort of miniature paradigm of the whole book. So do many other scenes producing the general effect of a calm after a storm—an effect especially notable after Goodwin's lynching, in the description of the flames "roaring silently out of a peaceful void." In the final pages everyone calms down and gives up. We are given no details of the lynching of Goodwin, since we see it only through Horace's eyes, and when Horace appeared on the scene Goodwin was presumably already dead. But from his wanting to get it over with that morning, we can assume that he accepted it stoically and perhaps with a sense of relief that he was not subjected to the delays of the law. For some time his main concern has been to restore Ruby's freedom to her before she is "too old to hustle a good man," and to make a minimal provision for a sickly son who will obviously not live long enough to need it.

The three main characters who surrender to apathy are Horace, Popeye, and Temple. As we have already seen, Horace really surrendered halfway through the trial; after the verdict he collapsed. He once again took orders from his sister, returned meekly to the domineering wife whom he had left a few days before the beginning of the novel, and resumed his incestuous velleities towards his stepdaughter. This collapse offers no real problem. He had started out to strike a blow for justice and decency, on the naive assumption that he must succeed because truth and justice are bound to triumph. Along the way he gradually sensed that things don't go that way in real life, and began to look forward to the defeat that would prove the vanity of idealistic struggle and let him give up, fall back, and stop bothering.

Even before the trial started, this had seemed the only solution for the problems of the world. When he left Miss Reba's, after interviewing Temple there, he thought of death for everyone involved in the case as the best that could be desired.

> And I too; thinking how that were the only solution. And I too, now that we're all isolated; thinking of a gentle dark wind blowing in the long corridors of sleep, of lying beneath a low cozy roof under the long sound of the rain: the evil, the injustice, the tears. . . . Perhaps it is upon the instant that we realize, admit, that there is a logical pattern to evil, that we die, he thought, thinking of the expression he had once seen in the eyes of a dead child, and of other dead: the cooling indignation, the shocked despair fading, leaving two empty globes in which the motionless world lurked profoundly in miniature.

The first part of this much-discussed passage makes it clear enough that Horace is miscast as a righter of the world's wrongs: what he really wants is peace and quiet. We can grant and even admire his admirable qualities, but his is a fugitive and cloistered virtue that cannot cope with the dust and heat. Realizing that there is a logical pattern to evil seems to mean realizing that it is not merely a superstition to be discredited or a spook to be exorcised, but a real and mighty force in the world's affairs and a greater force than his own genuine but ineffectual virtue. When we realize this we die, give up, surrender, and the figure of the expression in the eyes of the dead is profoundly significant. The indignation and despair of the original shock fade rapidly, leaving not acceptance or resignation or hope but mere emptiness, and the empty eyes of the dead give a reflection— both physically and metaphysically—of the world itself. This is the kernel of *Sanctuary*.

Ruby, for all her fine qualities, has seen the defeat coming, and accepted it fatalistically. The last we hear of her she is faithfully following Goodwin as far as she can, standing outside the jail to which he has been returned, with the child in her arms, " 'Standing where he can see it through the window,' Horace said." But she had long ago lost the will to resist. When she was trying to get Horace to dissociate himself from her and the case, she had told him, "I guess

I've got just what was coming to me. There's no use fighting it."

After winning every trick, Popeye simply throws in his hand. Thematically, his trial is an echo of Goodwin's and to some extent a parody of it. Popeye also has an ineffectual lawyer, this one assigned by the court. Like Goodwin, Popeye does not want bail and refuses to give his lawyer any information. In his case, too, a Memphis lawyer—it might even be the same one—shows up late in the proceedings. In both episodes there is a singing Negro in the jail. Once again the law takes its course of injustice, justifying its claim to "a certain clumsy stability in lieu of anything better" which is as much as Faulkner is willing to concede to it. He underlines the parallel between the two cases by reporting the outcome in two identical sentences: at the end of each trial "The jury was out eight minutes." It has been claimed that Popeye ironically cannot defend himself because he was actually killing Red at the time when he was supposed to have killed the Alabama policeman (Longley). The coincidence is certainly intended as an irony, but it is equally certain that it had nothing to do with Popeye's fate. He presumably killed Red shortly after Temple was led out of the roadhouse, and his presence there earlier that evening would have been an adequate alibi, even if proving an alibi had been the only possible defense. Popeye clearly acquiesces in his own death. Faulkner reminds us of the logical reasons for his conduct by describing him at the time of his arrest as

> that man who made money and had nothing he could do
> with it, spend it for, since he knew that alcohol would kill
> him like poison, who had no friends and had never known
> a woman and knew he could never.

This situation alone would be enough to make him (echoing Goodwin) tell the judge to "Get it over with all at once."

But Popeye is not the sort of man to base an indirect suicide on an analysis of his personal situation. It is true that Faulkner never takes us into Popeye's mind, and that we have no way of being certain what went on there during his trial and while he was awaiting execution. If I had to hazard a guess, I would say that he probably held a dialogue with himself running something like this: "Do you want to go on living?"—"No."—"Well, don't then," and that was all. But behind the immediate desire would lie a vague sense of the general meaninglessness of everything, and a bored indifference to both life and death.

We do not know just when Temple gives up. If we did, we might have a clearer understanding of her conduct at the trial. The difference in Faulkner's presentations of Temple and Popeye is interesting. Popeye is always treated as an object rather than a person: we are told what he said and did, but never what he thought or felt. The last episode of his life is really no more puzzling than any other, for he has always been an enigma. The account of his antecedents and childhood (added in the revision in galley proof) may give us some abstract comprehension of him as a case history, but it does not help in grasping him as a human being—if, indeed, he be one. When he is described on the second page as having "that vicious depthless quality of stamped tin," only his physical appearance is in question. But as the novel proceeds, we realize that the memorable phrase is a moral summary of his character. The two essential facts about Popeye are that he is consistently evil and that he is consistently presented as a two-dimensional character, from the spring at the Old Frenchman Place to the gallows in Alabama.

Temple is treated very differently. A large part of the action at Goodwin's, many of the scenes at Miss Reba's, and the flight from there and the events at the roadhouse leading up to the murder of Red are presented from her point of view. We are constantly installed as observers in her calculating, conceited little mind. But after Red is murdered we see her only twice—at the trial, and in the final scene in the Luxembourg Gardens, and both times she is treated entirely from the outside, as Popeye has been throughout the book. In the trial scene we have purely factual reporting. In the garden scene there are heavy emotional overtones provided by a consistent use of the pathetic fallacy from "that quality of autumn, gallant and evanescent and forlorn," near the beginning of the scene to "the season of rain and death" with which *Sanctuary* ends. But these are the comments of an omniscient narrator, applied to the scene and the situation in general, and we cannot take them as necessarily indicating Temple's state of mind. The simple fact is that we know practically nothing about her state of mind after the murder of Red.

We do know, however, that she has undergone a change and fallen into a state of apathy and, presumably, indifference. Earlier, she had been in constant, violent, and often purposeless motion, perpetually running and whirling and darting and leaping about. In

her last two appearances she is listless and inert. Earlier she had been
perpetually scheming and calculating, always on the make in one
way or another to achieve some usually vain or petty or momentary
aim. Now she seems utterly indifferent and aimless. Her last two acts
are to yawn (for the first and only time in the whole book) and to
perform what is for her the automatic, mechanical act of taking out
her compact and looking at herself, at a face "sullen and discontented
and sad"—but she has lost even the will to fiddle with her make-up.
And after this "she seemed to follow with her eyes the waves of
music," but note the *seemed*: even the omniscient narrator is not sure
of anything beyond the overt acts of yawning and opening and
closing the compact.

Everything seems to suggest that Temple, like Horace and
Popeye, but in her own way, has given up. Horace has abandoned
his idealism and returned to the trivial everyday details of a false and
meaningless life. Popeye's life has always been false and meaningless,
and he has given it up entirely. Temple has abandoned her flapper-
and-whorehouse scheming and fallen into total apathy. It is com-
monly said that she has learned nothing from her horrifying
experiences, and this is certainly true as far as any moral insight into
herself or the world is concerned. On the other hand, it might be
contended that she has learned the highest human wisdom, a sense of
the vanity of human wishes. But this would be going too far. She has
learned nothing, either morally or intellectually, but has simply
fallen into a state of lethargic indifference.

Temple has clearly followed the same path as the other principal
characters of *Sanctuary,* from active, self-centered confrontations to
indifference and apathy; and this is, of course, the pattern of the book
itself. The inevitable result is a profoundly pessimistic book, one that
has often been called Faulkner's most despairing and bitter work.
Few critics would quarrel with such a designation. The final position
reached by most of the characters, and apparently by the novel itself,
is that it—no matter what *it* is—simply does not matter, and such a
conclusion is, by normal human standards, one of despair. In many
ways, *Sanctuary* can be set alongside James Thomson's *The City of
Dreadful Night* as one of the most uncompromising expressions of
total despair in literature.

There are, however, two necessary qualifications of this view.
The first is that there is no great sense of loss because there has been
nothing much to lose. Horace Benbow's naive idealism and deter-

mination to make the right prevail are admirable in theory, but faintly ludicrous in practice, as well as ineffectual. Miss Jenny is too minor a character here to matter, and our admiration for her is largely carried over from *Sartoris*. Temple discovers and practices her propensity for evil, and for her to withdraw into apathy is a positive gain. So is the wiping out of Popeye: it is no more a tragedy than is the erasing of any other mistake.

The Goodwins represent the best that can be found in the world of *Sanctuary*. Lee is not what generally would be called an admirable man. He has a turbulent and violent nature, and has committed one murder in a sordid brawl over a wench. He beats Ruby on occasion, but he loves her in his fashion, and that is one of his ways of showing his love for her. He is genuinely concerned for her future when he foresees his own death, and there is no question that, with all his faults, he does have a certain fundamental human decency which is entirely lacking in such characters as Popeye, Temple, and Narcissa. Ruby is unquestionably the most admirable person in the novel. She is faithful to Lee by instinct, not on principle—in fact, she is puzzled by her own faithfulness. She has been a prostitute, so far as we specifically know, only for Lee's benefit, though Popeye implies that she has been an ordinary Memphis whore as well. But she does have conspicuous virtues, and she is permitted to keep them to the end, which for her is left open. Nevertheless, we must not lose our sense of proportion. Is Ruby Lamar really, on absolute human standards, a person of great value, or does she simply appear to be one, by contrast, in the sorry world of *Sanctuary*? In either case, her merits survive the action of the book and her story consequently does not produce any strong sense of loss.

The other qualification of *Sanctuary*'s despair depends on the reaction of the characters, the author, and the reader, to the final meaninglessness of the world which the book expresses. "It does last," Horace says. "Spring does. You'd almost think there was some purpose in it." This is after Goodwin's conviction, when Horace is a broken man, preparing to give up and go back to Belle. Coming from Horace, this is unquestionably a bitter observation. He has discovered that the world does not run to suit *his* purposes, and he somewhat childishly concludes that it therefore has no purpose of any kind. There is a good deal of this sort of petulance in much of the current literature and philosophy which assumes that the universe is absurd unless it makes man its spoiled darling. Most religions have traditionally hedged on the question: man must and should subordinate his desires to the will of a higher power, but this power made the universe for man, and man is a flawed copy of this power—and its spoiled darling as well.

If the world is supposed to hold and vindicate the values of Horace Benbow—and he clearly thinks that it is—then its failure to do so is a crushing blow. On the other hand, if one can admit himself to be only a small part of a world he never made and can give up the idea that it should conform to his desires and ideals, then accepting its indifference can become not a burden, but a release. Horace's final apathy says: It doesn't matter, and that's an outrage. But the next step would say: It doesn't matter that it doesn't matter.

Is this the stage reached by the final apathy of Popeye and Temple Drake? Probably not, in the form here proposed. Temple is not given to speculative thought, and though we know next to nothing about Popeye's mental processes, we can be sure that he is not philosophically inclined. But few people live by abstract concepts consciously analyzed. Most live by inchoate feelings and states of mind, and the final inertia of Temple and Popeye—a total indifference apparently untouched by any feeling of either outrage or regret—may well contain the essence of the formulation *it doesn't matter that it doesn't matter.*

I would certainly not insist that this is what Faulkner intended or that, regardless of his intentions, this is what the novel must mean. But Faulkner notoriously refuses to settle his issues, or even his plots, unequivocally. He regularly leaves various options open to his readers (hence the constant confrontations of his more dogmatic critics), and the interpretation which I have suggested is unquestionably one such option. If we choose it, *Sanctuary* ceases to be a novel of pessimism or despair, and becomes an expression of a sort of philosophical nihilism. And it makes more sense in the total work of Faulkner as the extreme point of the position towards which he had been moving since *Soldiers' Pay,* and from which he swung back after *Sanctuary* to an affirmation of human values.

Sanctuary and Dostoevsky

Jean Weisgerber

Less than a week after its appearance, John Chamberlain compared Faulkner's new novel to *The Brothers Karamazov* without developing the idea further. The idea was to be taken up again in 1959 by Edward Wasiolek, but the latter, far from believing in a profound influence, limits Dostoevsky's contribution to three passages by Faulkner. It appears, nonetheless, that a detailed examination of *Sanctuary* can bear more appreciable results.

The plot, or at least its most crucial moments, takes place indoors as is so often the case in Dostoevsky. The wind-and-rain-swept country crossed by the Bundrens is left in order to penetrate into a bootlegger's hideout, dilapidated rooms, a barn, a bordello, a bar, or a court room. The setting suffocates the characters by its tightness, ugliness, filth: everything here, like Raskolnikov's garret, indicates a separation from nature.

Sanctuary, in its general outline, recounts the same story as *Crime and Punishment* and *The Brothers Karamazov:* a serious infraction of the law (a murder accompanied by rape or theft) followed by an investigation and a trial. In the cases of Popeye and Raskolnikov, the reader is informed of the crime from the outset while he watches Goodwin's lawyer, Horace Benbow, and Porfiry, the examiner, attempt with great difficulty to reconstruct the facts. On the other

From *Faulkner and Dostoevsky: Influence and Confluence,* translated by Dean McWilliams. © 1974 by Ohio University Press.

hand, the role assigned to the trial in *Sanctuary* squares rather well with the episode described in book 12 of *The Brothers Karamazov*, "A Judicial Error." We shall see later that Faulkner was inspired by both novels at the same time.

Three scenes in *Sanctuary* are, in fact, more or less directly related to these novels. They are in ascending order of importance: the second part of chapter 24, the beginning of the next chapter, and chapters 27 and 28, passages which are all located near the end of the book. The first, the most distant from the supposed model, recounts the conversation of Popeye, Red and Temple at the dancehall: a banal situation of two rivals circling a woman disgusted by one of them and in love with the other. The circumstance recalls, in a general way, the scene at the inn in *The Brothers Karamazov* (bk. 8, chap. 8) during which the Pole and Dmitri give themselves over to "almost an orgy, a feast to which all were welcomed" in the company of Grushenka: the gaming table, the lascivious music, the woman's drunkenness and the awakening of desire, all of this is also noted by Faulkner. In chapter 25, we witness the consequences of the preceding scene, Red's funeral, a grotesque and macabre tableau showing a "disorderly and drunken crowd" and ending in a general uproar, like the long funeral banquet in *Crime and Punishment* (bk. 5, chaps. 2 and 3). But it is well known that naturalism thrived on such drinking bouts and, all things considered, nothing proves Dostoevsky's influence here.

Such is not the case with the trial of Goodwin (chaps. 27 and 28) the development of which follows book 12 of *The Brothers Karamazov* rather closely in its general outline. The situations, in fact, are in no way different. The guilty parties, Popeye and Smerdyakov, both portrayed as abnormal, do not even appear, and escape legal punishment, although the author repairs this injustice by disposing of them himself, while an innocent person, Goodwin or Dmitri, expiates in their place based on the dubious testimony of a woman (Temple, Katerina Ivanovna). The two writers thus demonstrate the incompatibility of morality and law, to which Dostoevsky adds the theme of redemption through suffering; in Faulkner evil and error triumph, without being able to transform themselves into good. In addition, there are some details which correspond. Just as Goodwin begins by concealing Popeye's presence at the scene of the murder from Horace, his lawyer, so also does Dmitri initially refuse to furnish the prosecutor with explanations that might clear him; their motives, although different, lead to an analogous conduct. The trial itself, which occupies all of the last book of *The Brothers Karamazov* (around a hundred pages) is in *Sanctuary* reduced to a short chapter (chap. 28) and to two fragments of the preceding one: in all about ten pages. In addition to the indictment and the defense which he recounts in detail, Dostoevsky speaks in book 11 of Grushenka and Alyosha's visits to Dmitri in prison awaiting the judgement. If, in *Sanctuary,* Temple's accusation and testimony are brief, the visit takes on greater importance. We watch the accused, his mistress (Ruby) and his lawyer reunited in the cell, but because he wishes to underline Horace's weakness and not to regenerate Goodwin, Faulkner plunges the latter in a deep sleep while Horace rehearses Ruby in her role for the fatal day, an effort which proves fruitless. The visit cuts the trial scene in two, dividing the two days over which it is spread; in Dostoevsky the trial develops in a single, unbroken movement. With the exception of this difference, the ceremonial is identical: the introduction of evidence, the description of the room, the appearance of witnesses, the duel of the defense and prosecution, the decisive role of the jury, and the rapidity of deliberations: "exactly an hour, neither more nor less" for the Russian, a mere eight minutes for the American. The essential similarity is obviously the sudden change produced by defense witnesses, Temple and Katerina Ivanovna, who quite unexpectedly crush the accused by consciously lying. In both cases the material proofs which support their statements and reflect two social taboos, that is, a young girl's virginity and a father's life, are isolated from the circumstances to which they originally belonged. The corn cob, the instrument of rape, was not used by Goodwin, whose virility precludes such artifices, but by Popeye, an impotent voyeur. As for Dmitri's letter announcing that he is going to kill his father, which is introduced by Katerina, it was written while in an inebriated state. Finally, as if to accentuate the irony of the judgement, Popeye is executed for a murder he did not commit and Smerdyakov hangs himself. True justice takes it revenge in the end, thanks to the novelist's good will and not by means of the tribunal whose blindness and futility is denounced. It is, moreover, a pyrrhic victory: the innocent are punished along with the guilty, and the instigator gets off free. Morally, in any case, Ivan and Temple bear a good portion of the responsibility: Smerdyakov does no more than put into practice ill-digested theories, and Popeye succumbs, like so many others, to the blandishments of an eighteen-year-old Eve. Once more, the value and the relations of the characters are modified in passing from one book to another. It is, for example, impossible to confuse Katerina Ivanovna, Dmitri's former fiancee, and Temple Drake, who scarcely knows Goodwin: the two women have nothing in common except their perjury. But in *Sanctuary* the role of traitor falls not only to Temple: she shares it with Narcissa, the lawyer's sister, who—following Katerina's example—sells the accused to save the being dearest to her. Narcissa aids the prosecution out of love for her brother (or his respectability), Katerina to cover Ivan. Thus the Dostoevskian heroine is dismembered, Temple and Narcissa together fulfilling the function assigned to Katerina Ivanovna alone.

In addition to the trial, one discovers a host of even more precise analogies in the situations and reactions of the characters.

Temple, hunted down and raped at gunpoint by Popeye (chap. 13), surpasses Dounia of *Crime and Punishment,* whose virtue barely triumphs over Svidrigailov's importunities (bk. 6, chap. 5). The latter, as we know, courts a young maiden: "a girl who'll be sixteen in another month" who sometimes "steals a look at [him] that positively scorches [him]"; Temple—"her eyes blankly right and left looking, cool, predatory and discreet"—is not much older, although infinitely more dangerous. Her long confession to Horace (chap. 23) could have developed from those loved by Dostoevsky; in any case, it contains a direct borrowing from *Crime and Punishment.* She explains that during the night while Popeye handled her, she believed herself dead:

> I could see myself in the coffin. I looked sweet—you know: all in white. I had on a veil like a bride, and I was crying because I was dead or looked sweet or something. No: it was because they had put shucks in the coffin.

Minus the details, it is precisely the dream that Svidrigailov had before his suicide:

> On a table covered with a white satin shroud, stood a coffin. The coffin was covered with white silk and edged with a thick white frill; wreaths of flowers surrounded it on all sides. Among the flowers lay a girl in a white muslin dress, with her arms crossed and pressed on her bosom, as though carved out of marble. But her loose fair hair was wet; there was a wreath of roses on her head. The stern and

already rigid profile of her face looked as though chiselled of marble too, and the smile on her pale lips was full of an immense unchildish misery and sorrowful appeal.

To be sure the meanings diverge: that which in the Russian novel is meant to express the criminal's remorse, in *Sanctuary* takes on the victim's anguish. Nonetheless, the image of the dead young girl, although seen from opposite angles, remains linked to the theme of rape.

All of this chapter (bk. 6, chap. 6) seems to have made a vivid impression on Faulkner, for one finds its traces in two other places in *Sanctuary*, already pointed out by Wasiolek. Just after his first dream, Svidrigailov encounters in a "long narrow corridor . . . a little girl, not more than five years old" whom he cares for like a mother. Leaning over her once she is asleep, he sees her pure features twist into a lewd grimace:

> He suddenly fancied that her long black eyelashes were quivering, as though the lids were opening and a sly crafty eye peeped out with an unchildlike wink, as though the little girl were not asleep, but pretending. Yes, it was so. Her lips parted in a smile. The corners of her mouth quivered, as though she were trying to control them. But now she quite gave up all effort, now it was a grin, a broad grin; there was something shameless, provocative in that quite unchildish face; it was depravity, it was the face of a harlot, the shameless face of a French harlot. Now both eyes opened wide; they turned a glowing, shameless glance upon him; they laughed, invited him. . . . There was something infinitely hideous and shocking in that laugh, in those eyes, in such nastiness in the face of a child. "What, at five years old?" Svidrigailov muttered in genuine horror. "What does it mean?" And now she turned to him, her little face all aglow, holding out her arms . . . "Accursed child!" Svidrigailov cried, raising his hand to strike her, but at that moment he woke up.

Horace assists at the same metamorphosis while he contemplates the photograph of Little Belle, the daughter born of his wife's first marriage. The first time in chapter 19:

He moved, suddenly. As of its own accord the photograph had shifted, slipping a little from its precarious balancing against the book. The image blurred into the highlight, like something familiar seen beneath disturbed though clear water: he looked at the familiar image with a kind of quiet horror and despair, at a face suddenly older in sin than he would ever be, a face more blurred than sweet, at eyes more secret than soft.

A second time at the end of chapter 23, the chapter in which Temple has already just taken an image from Svidrigailov's nightmare:

The photograph sat on the dresser. He took it up, holding it in his hands. Enclosed by the narrow imprint of the missing frame Little Belle's face dreamed with that quality of sweet chiaroscuro. Communicated to the cardboard by some quality of the light or perhaps by some infinitesimal movement of his hands, his own breathing, the face appeared to breathe in his palms in a shallow bath of highlight, beneath the slow, smoke-like tongues of invisible honeysuckle. Almost palpable enough to be seen, the scent filled the room and the small face seemed to swoon in a voluptuous languor, blurring still more, fading, leaving upon his eye a soft and fading aftermath of invitation and voluptuous promise and secret affirmation like a scent itself.

Wasiolek shows very clearly that the heroes experience an identical disgust before the transformation of innocence into lasciviousness, an imaginary "fall" that is accomplished either in a dream or by an optical illusion caused by the lighting. In his view, the passage indicates a moment of awareness: Svidrigailov, after reading his own lewdness on the child's face, puts a bullet in his brain; Horace, for his part, could conclude with the apostle that all of the world is under the power of evil. Such is, moreover, the central idea of the book, in which Temple applies the reflections of Lise and Alyosha in *The Brothers Karamazov* literally: "I want to do evil . . . there are moments when people love crime" (*Karamazov*).

Little Belle is not the only child about which Horace is concerned. The image of Ruby's sickly nurseling, glimpsed at the beginning, accompanies him like a reproach, similar to the obsession from which Ivan Karamazov suffered. The arguments the latter develops for the benefit of Alyosha (bk. 5, chap. 4, "Rebellion") are well known: how does one understand, justify, accept the suffering of these young innocents who have not eaten of the forbidden fruit and yet "must suffer for their fathers' sins." In Faulkner, despite the absence of any religious nuance, the child is nonetheless defined similarly as condemned to suffer in a way that is absurd, irremediable and, therefore, revolting. Horace, without posing as a philosopher reacts like Ivan (chap. 16), but the menacing presence that crushes innocence, far from resulting from the imponderable decrees of God, is here materialized in the person of Popeye, the instrument of Evil.

> [Horace] looking down at the child, at its bluish eyelids showing a faint crescent of bluish white against its lead-colored cheeks, the moist shadow of hair capping its skull, its hands uplifted, curl-palmed, sweating too, thinking Good God. Good God.
>
> He was thinking of the first time he had seen it, lying in a wooden box behind the stove in that ruined house twelve miles from town; of Popeye's black presence lying upon the house like a shadow of something no larger than a match falling monstrous and portentous upon something else otherwise familiar and everyday and twenty times its size; of the two of them—himself and the woman—in the kitchen lighted by a cracked and smutty lamp on a table of clean, spartan dishes and Goodwin and Popeye somewhere in the outer darkness peaceful with insects and frogs yet filled too with Popeye's presence in black and nameless threat.

And it is again the same passage from *The Brothers Karamazov* whose echo one perceives in a dialogue between Horace and Miss Jenny. Horace delivers himself of a violent diatribe against society and the Church which, stigmatizing murder and adultery—crimes of which Goodwin is guilty in their eyes—would put the parents to death and take charge of their illegitimate child in order to raise him in the terror of sin.

> Then they all jumped on him [Goodwin]. The good customers, that had been buying whiskey from him and drinking all that he would give them free and maybe trying to make love to his wife behind his back. You should hear them down town. This morning the Baptist

minister took him for a text. Not only as a murderer, but as an adulterer; a polluter of the free Democratico-Protestant atmosphere of Yoknapatawpha county. I gathered that his idea was that Goodwin and the woman should both be burned as a sole example to that child; the child to be reared and taught the English language for the sole end of being taught that it was begot in sin by two people who suffered by fire for having begot it. Good God, can a man, a civilised man, seriously . . .

Horace thus tears away the Christian garments in which his fellow citizens have dressed themselves. In Jefferson, the concern for respectability and the desire for vengeance have smothered love for one's neighbor. Brothers have become tormentors; charity, indifferent to misery, is used only to judge and torture. This is precisely what Ivan explained to Alyosha when he told him about the execution in Geneva:

Five years ago, a murderer, Richard, was executed—a young man, I believe, of three and twenty, who repented and was converted to the Christian faith at the very scaffold. This Richard was an illegitimate child who was given as a child of six by his parents to some shepherds on the Swiss mountains. They brought him up to work for them. . . . Richard had been given to them as a chattel, and they did not even see the necessity of feeding him. . . . he lived like a brute and finished by killing and robbing an old man. He was caught, tried, and condemned to death. They are not sentimentalists there. And in prison he was immediately surrounded by pastors, members of Christian brotherhoods, philanthropic ladies and the like. They taught him to read and write in prison, and expounded the Gospel to him. They exhorted him, worked upon him, drummed at him incessantly, till at last he solemnly confessed his crime. He was converted. He wrote to the court himself that he was a monster, but that in the end God had vouchsafed him light and shown grace. All Geneva was in excitement about him—all philanthropic and religious Geneva. All the aristocratic and well-bred society of the town rushed to the prison, kissed Richard and embraced him; "You are our brother, you have found grace. . . ." And so, covered with his brothers' kisses, Richard is dragged to the scaffold and led to the guillotine. And they chopped off his head in brotherly fashion because he had found grace.

Faulkner condenses the story and tones down the irony. However, if Horace does not "admit" the world any more than Ivan, his attack is directed less against the Creator than against the creatures: Yoknapatawpha, its laws, morality, churches. It is appropriate to add to Wasiolek's pertinent commentary that the story of Richard immediately precedes that of the "little horse" which Faulkner reworked (?) in *Sartoris*. Of all the episodes in *The Brothers Karamazov*, "Rebellion" takes on a major significance around 1930: stripped of its metaphysical implications, it could serve as an epigraph for the denunciations of Southern society and its violence that are to be found in *Sanctuary* and *Light in August*.

In addition to these, the most convincing of the analogies, other details also strike the reader. Miss Reba, the madam of the bordello in which Popeye, Temple and Red amuse themselves, seems to borrow several traits from the madam of *Crime and Punishment*—her "very stout, buxom" figure, her "glittering jewels" ("the other hand ringed with yellow diamonds as large as gravel, lost among the lush billows of her breast"), her sense of bourgeois propriety, and finally her comic appearance. But nothing can be inferred from the traditional attributes of this literary type; none of this denotes a direct filiation. The same remark can be made about Ruby, Goodwin's mistress and devoted servant—one need not be influenced by *Crime and Punishment* and Sonia Marmeladov, in particular, to sacrifice everything for someone one loves. It is not so much the resemblances, in themselves imprecise and perhaps accidental, which bestow a Dostoevskian stamp on *Sanctuary* as their accumulation. And then they are not limited to such futile details. The splitting of the personality which afflicts successively Horace and Temple, the use of a leitmotif such as the rouged lips and cheeks of Temple, the opposition established between the Christian facade and true charity: does one not recognize here, more or less confusedly, Ivan Karamazov's hallucinations, Svidrigailov's careful appearance and one of the themes of "Rebellion"?

Sanctuary's dependence on Dostoevsky is probably less extensive than that of *The Sound and the Fury*. But the links, although fewer, are also tighter.

Sanctuary and Faulkner's Misogyny

Albert J. Guerard

Sanctuary is much underrated, partly because of Faulkner's grossly misleading comment that it was a potboiler written in a few weeks, but also because it is so unlike the "greatest" Faulkners; seems to lack the manifest seriousness of *Light in August, The Sound and the Fury, Absalom, Absalom!* and *The Bear,* as well as their difficulty. *Sanctuary* belongs more than most of Faulkner's novels to a recognizable mode of American writing: the tough tight compassionate grotesque picture of suffering, depravity, defeat. There is no redemption in *Sanctuary* other than the redemption of art. The vision is at best one of stoic defeatism, but concludes in despair and a recognition of the void: Horace returning to the horror of life with Belle; Popeye refusing to appeal his absurd sentence; Temple yawning in the Luxembourg Gardens, in the season of rain and death. (The Temple of *Requiem for a Nun* is an altogether different person in an implausible "new life.") The relatively short sentences and objective narration and laconic dialogue may remind us of Hemingway. But the truer affinity is with Flaubert, distancing vulgarity through poetic detail and serenely composed syntax. *Sanctuary* is what Dostoevsky would have called, I think, a *poem.* Meanness and evil and depravity, *seen as such* and with precision, but seen also with compassion, constitute a work of beauty, precisely as does Toulouse-Lautrec's painting of an ugly middle-aged prostitute wearily raising her shift.

From *The Triumph of the Novel: Dickens, Dostoevsky, Faulkner.* © 1976 by Albert J. Guerard. Oxford University Press, 1976.

Far more than with Dickens and Dostoevsky, the obsession was put to artistic use. Faulkner's misogyny, that is, gave form, solidity, energy to a general vision of contemporary depravity and timeless evil. But *Sanctuary* is a picture, not merely a "vision," of the contemporary depravity, specifically of north Mississippi, more generally of prohibition America. A real lynching occurred at the Oxford courthouse, several years after the publication of *Sanctuary*, and Memphis with its gang conflicts was known as Murder Capital of the U.S.A. The real life contrast for Faulkner was not merely between his somnolent college town and Memphis (where he enjoyed exploring the fringe world of entertainment and corruption) but between the daily tedium of Lafayette/Yoknapatawpha county and its sporadic outbreaks of violence. The "jazz age" students and the resentful townies, Gowan Stevens and his pride in his drinking, the delegation of women protesting Ruby Lamar's stay at the hotel— these are not figures of fantasy, though this might be said of the millionaire lawyer, weighing 280 pounds, who has installed his special bed in Miss Reba's establishment, or the police commissioner discovered there, naked and dancing the Highland Fling. At a fine line between documentary realism and soaring fictional vision stands Senator Clarence Snopes, whose twin brothers Vardaman and Bilbo were named after well-known Mississippi politicians. The soiled hat and greasy velvet collar and "majestic sweep of flesh on either side of a small blunt nose" would have been at home in Dickens's London. He is persona non grata at Miss Reba's for feeling the girls' behinds while spending nothing: " 'Look here, mister, folks what uses this waiting-room has got to get on the train now and then.' " The Memphis depravities (except for Temple's) reach us refracted by the grotesque, or by Miss Reba's comic vision, but also by Clarence Snopes's cupidity and cynical humor. Thus the bas-fonds misery and exploitation of the negro whorehouse he leads the young innocents to, lest they spend three dollars again:

> "Them's niggers," Virgil said.
> " 'Course they're niggers," Clarence said. "But see this?" he waved a banknote in his cousin's face. "This stuff is color-blind."

Miss Reba's establishment, except for Temple's room, seems a place of good-humored innocence. Virgil's and Fonzo's classic mistake, and their own innocence sustained for so long, adds to a familiar iconography that tempted even Gide in *Lafcadio's Adventures*. Red's funeral, only a slight parodic extension of gangster ceremonies of the twenties, is also kept at a comic distance. This is but to say that Memphis, the legendary Babylon for north Mississippians, is appropriately stylized. But the "normal" depravities and deprivations of the Old Frenchman Place, running to ruin and jungle, are intensely real: the slaving Ruby with her sickly child in the box, fiercely cursing; the blind and deaf old man edging his chair into the sun; the mattress of shucks and that other bed of corncobs and cottonseed hulls and the barn loft with its rat. The four men move in somnambulistic, mechanical lust in the room where Temple stands terrified in the corner and the bloody Gowan lies on the mattress. Later the room is in a darkness where Tommy's pale eyes glow faintly, like a cat's, and Popeye's presence is known from the odor of brilliantine. The scenes are taut, spare, intensely real: great dramatic writing.

Interwoven with the general depravity, the picture of the time and place, is Faulkner's deeper vision of evil embodied in the impotent Popeye and the amoral Temple in her nervous animal lust. Theirs is a more than ordinary, "normal" corruption. Popeye reaches us in part through traditional symbolism: evil as blackness, as hollowness, as mechanism. Faulkner like Melville knew the power of blackness, Benito Cereno's sense of "the negro" as a spiritual coloring, though in the 1970s he might have used a different language. Popeye is in fact white, of a "queer, bloodless color"; Temple's early reference to him as that "black man" is a response to the incongruous black suit, which becomes a kind of mask, the accouterment of his gangster role and an assertion of identity. Popeye is simply, as Benbow talks to Narcissa and Miss Jenny, "that little black man." But in a later passage the blackness is generalized: a "black presence lying upon the house like the shadow of something no larger than a match falling monstrous and portentous upon something else otherwise familiar and twenty times its size."

Popeye is, even more than Conrad's Kurtz or James Wait, a hollow man, bereft of any inner humanity to help him confront the void. He *is* his black suit, his slanting straw hat, his cigarette, his gun; he is his role, perhaps learned from movies as well as life, of a gangster people are afraid of. He is also the mechanical man, composed of inanimate parts, with doll-like hands and eyes "two knobs of soft black rubber," "the face of a wax doll set too near a hot fire," bloodless, and with "the vicious depthless quality of stamped tin." The first compelling image is of inexplicable evil and gratuitous terrorism, as for two hours the squatting Popeye watches Horace across the spring. Through much of the Frenchman Place section his malice remains shadowy, enigmatic: a pleasureless need to control, humiliate, scorn. The murder of Tommy, coldly casual, disposes of a minor irritant and is punishment for minor disobedience; the murder of Red follows upon a passionless presentation, to Temple, of alternatives. But the evil becomes more meaningful as it is traced to Popeye's impotence. For the relationship of spiritual impotence to individual and collective violence is sociological and psychological reality. Popeye cannot even drink. His only pleasures are smoking and wearing the black suits of his terrorist's role; and the sadistic voyeurism. The voyeurism, the cerebration of sexuality and conversion of thwarted impulse into gesture and sound, is at once an emblem of inhumanity and sad psychological fact. Minutes before the corncob rape, watching Temple, Popeye "began to thrust his chin out in a series of jerks"; the shooting of Tommy on so little provocation, moments later, may be a first substitute for sexual act. Later, at the brothel, Miss Minnie will see Temple and Red naked as two snakes with Popeye above them making a whinnying sound. But we have already seen, unforgettably, the nervous displacement on his first visit to Temple in the brothel, Popeye crouched "beside the bed, his face wrung above his absent chin, his bluish lips protruding as though he were blowing upon hot soup, making a high whinnying sound like a horse."

The final chapter attempts, with some success, the turnabout of sympathy so effective with Joe Christmas, Thomas Sutpen, Mink Snopes: the revelation of childhood and later deprivation and trauma as cause. There has been some criticism of Popeye's acceptance of the death sentence "for killing a man in one town and at an hour when he was in another town killing somebody else," his refusal to appeal. But these pages are very moving, and Popeye in his cell is one of the loneliest of the many solitaries in American fiction—the "man who made money and had nothing he could do with it, spend it for," and whose last demands are for cigarettes and hair-lotion. The pages have some resemblance to the final ones of *The Stranger*. But unlike Meursault Popeye can take no comfort from the void, and the benign indifference of things; he experiences the void without recognizing that it exists. He merely smokes while the minister prays, where Meursault has his healing burst of rage.

My assumption is sufficiently unusual as to bear repetition: that Faulkner's misogyny, a tendentious attitude consciously indulged in *Sanctuary,* acted as a controlling, selective influence, very much as did the determination to write a spare, objective, nominally impersonal narrative, one relatively free of comment on the thoughts and feelings of the characters. In this his dual strategy had real affinity with Flaubert's in *Madame Bovary* and even more with that of Conrad in *The Secret Agent,* who restricted himself to a bleak vision of London as a slimy aquarium, with its anarchists and policemen essentially kin, and restricted himself too to a coldly ironic, deglamorized style. This is not to say that Faulkner's denigrative view of women was "insincere" in *Sanctuary,* only that it was more than usually unrelieved. The misogyny was not diffuse and compulsive, as often in the early Conrad, but recognized and accepted. Thus the letter to his editor Hal Smith, in which he tells of his "book about a girl who gets raped with a corn cob" and of "how all this evil flowed off her like water off a duck's back." Or, still more succinctly: "Women are completely impervious to evil" (Blotner).

The misogyny can take different forms, as we see if we compare the Narcissa of *Sanctuary* with her portrait in *Sartoris,* where she is, for Horace, the urnlike and unravished bride of quietness. Now, instead, she has the "serene and stupid impregnability of heroic statuary." She is stupid enough to tolerate Gowan Stevens but highly efficient in her betrayal of her brother's secret to the District Attorney. She may be a plausible rendering of a Southern woman of good family of her time: "I cannot have my brother mixed up with a woman people are talking about." But convention is carried very far when she says she can't see what difference it makes who committed the murder. "The question is, are you going to stay mixed up with it?" We know that Temple is willing to see an innocent man die. But so too is Narcissa, if only by selective inattention.

The changes in Little Belle, from *Sartoris,* are perhaps the normal ones brought by years. For the child whose "eyes were like stars, more soft and melting than any deer's," has changed for Horace, who now hears "the delicate and urgent mammalian whisper of that curious small flesh which he had not begot and in which appeared to be vatted delicately some seething sympathy with the blossoming grape." He stares "with a kind of quiet horror and despair, at a face suddenly older in sin than he would ever be, a face more blurred than sweet, at eyes more secret than soft." Little Belle, who picks up a man on a train, would seem to owe something both to the daughter Quentin and, as the incestuous fantasy associated with honeysuckle suggests, to Caddy. But no traumatic memory or fantasy of Caddy's brother is as terrible as Horace's, as Little Belle blends into Temple, while the "shucks set up a terrific uproar beneath her thighs." After hearing Temple's story, and as he approaches the house, where he will look at Little Belle's photograph, Horace has a vivid apprehension of the void, Conrad's cooling, dying world: "a world left stark and dying above the tide-edge of the fluid in which it lived and breathed. The moon stood overhead, but without light; the earth lay beneath, without darkness."

The vulgarity of the college girls is unrelieved, as they trade secrets of sexual attraction and prepare for the dance, the air "steamy with recent baths, and perhaps powder in the light like chaff in barn-lofts"; the barn connects them with Temple. The fierce vulgarity of Ruby Lamar is another matter, and the novel's view of her ambivalent. She is loyal, courageous, indestructible, but with some of Charlotte Rittenmeyer's frightening forthrightness. The narrating consciousness would seem to share Horace Benbow's horror over her blunt offer of herself in payment, this in turn not unlike Gavin Stevens's dismay with Eula and later Linda Snopes.

Miss Reba, however, exists in a sphere above and beyond questions of misogyny or moral judgment, and in this is like Sairey Gamp, to whom she may well be indebted. Her memories of life with Mr. Binford, the "two doves" now symbolized by two angry and wormlike dogs, have some of the quality of Sairey's fantasies, though Mr. Binford will, in *The Reivers,* have a material reality. The Miss Reba of *Sanctuary*—ample, commanding, humorous, loquacious—is intimately connected with the dogs, as they moil at her feet, snapping, or are kicked away. They share her asthmatic life, "climbing and sprawling onto the bed and into Miss Reba's lap with wheezy, flatulent sounds, billowing into the rich pneumasis of her breast and tonguing along the metal tankard which she waved in one ringed hand as she talked." She has her fine fictions, as does Sairey, of what is due her profession: "Me trying to run a respectable house, that's been running a shooting-gallery for thirty years, and him trying to turn it into a peep-show." She has her practical realism, assures Temple her maiden blood will be worth a thousand dollars to her, and drinks to the devirgination. The prose, with a macabre precision worthy of Flaubert, comments ironically on the event by describing the drawn shades:

> She lifted the tankard, the flowers on her hat rigidly moribund, nodding in macabre was hael. "Us poor girls," she said. The drawn shades, cracked into a myriad pattern like old skin, blew faintly on the bright air, breathing into the room on waning surges the sound of Sabbath traffic, festive, steady, evanescent.

Miss Reba is, like Sairey, an indestructible natural force.

Temple Drake is one of Faulkner's finest brief creations. A casual reader might see her as a run-of-the-mill "flapper" of her time, driven swiftly to nymphomania by the traumatic incident of unnatural rape. (In fact, she is unaware until later of what happened: "You couldn't fool me but once, could you?") Instead she is, as Flaubert saw Emma Bovary, "naturally corrupt," and like Emma comes to take the initiative with her lover and issues her sexual commands. Gowan Stevens, the Frenchman Place, Memphis simply help her realize her potentialities, which are already indicated by her name on the lavatory wall. She is the good petter, the demi-vierge and teaser known for saying, presumably at the moment of truth, "My father's a judge." Two of her protective fantasies before the rape suggest the sexual content of past reveries: she hopes to turn into a boy and to have a chastity belt. The third, to be a veiled bride in a coffin, all in white, may recall Svidrigaïlov's victim as well as Emma's nostalgic reveries of past innocence. But Temple differs radically from Emma, whose provocations were certainly more severe (the two villages and the dull husband), and whose sensuality had its poetry of delicate appearance and romantically dissolving will. Flaubert was, notoriously, ambivalent, and even shared the reveries he scorned. But the portrait of Temple in the taut *Sanctuary* is unequivocal and unredeemed.

The insistent denigrative imagery is remarkably effective. Temple is a mechanical being at the trial, dressed in the role of the gangster's moll. But in other major scenes she is an alert and savage animal, generally a cat: mindlessly springing (into cars and off a train, onto and off the porch, out of the crib and back in), running in animal fear, crouching and writhing, pausing, returning in animal heat. At Miss Reba's she turns restlessly in a littered cage. In the barn loft she is both a girl frightened of rats and herself a cornered rat. But eventually it is the real rat, who has just leaped at her head, that is terrified by the larger animal presence. Its squeaking functions, after a first reading, as brilliant anticipation of Popeye's helpless animal sounds:

> The rat was in that corner now, on the floor. Again their faces were not twelve inches apart, the rat's eyes glowing and fading as though worked by lungs. Then it stood erect, its back to the corner, its forepaws curled against its chest, and began to squeak at her in tiny plaintive gasps.

The female animal that runs from the house and back wants to be caught. The pattern is set as she gives Tommy one of her slippers to hold ("Durn ef I could git ere two of my fingers into one of them things . . . Kin I look at em?") but jerks her skirt down and springs up when she finds him looking at her lifted thigh. She has been told by Ruby to get away before dark, and is terrified of Popeye, yet is drawn two ways by feline nerves: "Temple met Popeye halfway to the house. Without ceasing to run she appeared to pause. Even her flapping coat did not overtake her, yet for an appreciable instant she faced Popeye with a grimace of taut, toothed coquetry." As real danger looms Temple wedges a chair against the door, but suddenly springs to her feet and takes off her dress, "crouching a little, match-thin in her scant undergarments." The divergent animal impulses to flee and to be caught turn to submission at Miss Reba's. She has played her game with the doctor, holding the covers to her throat. After he has left she springs from the bed and bolts the door. But presently, with fantasies of waiting for a date at home, she gets up and looks at herself in the mirror, at first seeing nothing, then "her breast rising out of a dissolving pall beneath which her toes peeped in pale, fleet intervals as she walked." She unbolts the door through which the two terrified dogs will presently come, to cower under the bed, and later in the evening Popeye.

The dissolving pall might have been imagined by Flaubert; elsewhere too, in this scene, delicate imagery comments in his manner on the sexuality which has become Temple's whole life. We return, several pages after the cracked shade associated with Miss

Reba's toast to her maiden blood, to that shade, with everything else now eroticized:

> In the window the cracked shade, yawning now and then with a faint rasp against the frame, let twilight into the room in fainting surges. From beneath the shade the smoke-colored twilight emerged in slow puffs like signal smoke from a blanket, thickening in the room. The china figures which supported the clock gleamed in hushed smooth flexions: knee, elbow, flank, arm and breast in attitudes of voluptuous lassitude. The glass face, become mirror-like, appeared to hold all reluctant light, holding in its tranquil depths a quiet gesture of moribund time, one-armed like a veteran from the wars.

The passage both conveys Temple's consciousness, her drowsing movement toward acceptance (in the next paragraph she will unbolt the door) and, with the last clause, comments ironically on it and on Popeye's impotence as well. Later in the chapter a passage justly admired by Cleanth Brooks, who sees it as relentlessly exposing "the pretentious sleaziness of the room," is also effective for its specifically sexual imagery. A paragraph that begins with imagery of enveloped sexual penetration ends with a slop jar, also enveloped:

> The light hung from the center of the ceiling, beneath a fluted shade of rose-colored paper browned where the bulb bulged it. . . . In the corner, upon a faded scarred strip of oilcloth tacked over the carpet, sat a washstand bearing a flowered bowl and pitcher and a row of towels; in the corner behind it sat a slop jar dressed also in fluted rose-colored paper.

Temple's imaginative anticipation of the rape, as she evokes it for Horace, is a triumph of artistic tact. There is expert modulation from her first simple sentences to efficient narration and imagery of great precision. She conveys her intense ambivalence, dreading and wanting the rape, and suggests persuasively, though indirectly, appalling physical detail. The picture of the completed nymphomania, as we see it at the Grotto and in the room she has commandeered, on the night of Red's death, is conveyed through imagery suggesting a death of her own. Once again there are affinities with Emma

Bovary: "shuddering waves of physical desire," the eyeballs drawn "back into her skull in a shuddering swoon":

> Her eyes began to grow darker and darker, lifting into her skull above a half moon of white, without focus, with the blank rigidity of a statue's eyes. She began to say Ah-ah-ah-ah in an expiring voice, her body arching slowly backward as though faced by an exquisite torture. When he touched her she sprang like a bow, hurling herself upon him, her mouth gaped and ugly like that of a dying fish as she writhed her loins against him.

The passage is echoed briefly as she leaves the trial, moving toward the four young men, bodyguards presumably employed by Popeye: "She began to cringe back, her body arching slowly, her arm tautening in the old man's grasp."

The measure of willed evil, as opposed to ordinary depravity and sexual neurosis, is taken twice, as she condemns first Red, then Lee Goodwin to death. She may for a time be under the illusion that Red has some chance for survival, when she telephones to make the assignation, but Popeye sees it as a free choice: " 'I'm giving him his chance,' he said, in his cold soft voice. 'Come on. Make up your mind.' " The risk seems to her worth taking. (*Requiem for a Nun*'s reimagining of this incident radically reduces her guilt.) Her perjury at the trial is unexcited, and like that of a drugged person. The imagery of fish returns: "Above the ranked intent faces white and pallid as the floating bellies of dead fish, she sat in an attitude at once detached and cringing, her gaze fixed on something at the back of the room." Her gazing recurs three times in the short scene. She is perhaps terrified by the bodyguards who, whether hired by Popeye or Eustace Graham, would remind her of the real murderer. But in a larger sense she seems to be gazing past the once familiar world, with its pretenses of order and legality, the world of the baseball game she had wanted to see, into the discovered world of evil; and beyond it into a void.

As Flaubert took commonplace and boring "material" and of it made a thing of beauty, so Faulkner with the sordid and mean; the violent, corrupt, depraved. Corresponding to *Sanctuary*'s ironic, pessimistic, insistently misogynous vision was a willed tautness of narrative method and style. The compression, by no means as natural to Faulkner as to Hemingway or Flaubert, was a source of energizing intensity; the author felt, as the reader feels, the presence of what is left out. The narrative compression is in places extraordinary. Goodwin's trial has only one short chapter and a few paragraphs more; the aftermath of the trial and the lynching even less. (The lynching is merely alluded to in an earlier version.) The poignant evocation of Popeye's background and diseased, neurotic childhood has a few pages only; his trial and the verdict three sentences, less than a hundred words. His jury, like Goodwin's, is out eight minutes. The spare narrative of Popeye awaiting death, quietly and as though indifferently, is as moving as that of Wilbourne in *The Wild Palms,* whose reflections reach us in a rich rhetoric—the one marking his days with cigarette stubs, the other pinching the cyanide tablet in a folded cigarette paper into powder and emptying it on the floor, since between grief and nothing he has elected grief, and fifty years in the penitentiary.

The plot may have been "horrific," in Faulkner's scornful word, but the most violent events are treated very briefly, or merely suggested, or omitted altogether. The death of Tommy comes with a sound "no louder than the striking of a match: a short, minor sound shutting down upon the scene, the instant, with a profound finality, completely isolating it." And the rape in the next paragraph is distanced for us by Temple's act of self-displacement, which has her tossing and thrashing not in the crib but on the rough, sunny boards outside, beneath the blind and deaf old man. Her harrowing account to Benbow does not reach the rape. She hints at some instrument, in raging at Popeye, but the corncob is revealed, and then most briefly, only at the trial. The traumatic doctor's examination, at Miss Reba's, occurs between paragraphs; Red's murder between chapters. The movement of the narrative is so swift that little room is left the reader for prurient imaginings.

The compression also obviated the interiority that Faulkner found so tempting, and that does threaten *Sanctuary* when Benbow is on the scene. The account of Temple and Gowan at the Old Frenchman Place (chaps. 5–14) is a triumph of spare, objective, nominally impersonal narration, as free of characters' thoughts and named feelings as any novel of Hemingway. We have a few laconic mutterings of Tommy, and a few short sentences on the reflections of the disgraced Gowan. Of Temple's interior torment almost nothing is "told." "Now I can stand anything, she thought quietly, with a kind of dull, spent astonishment; I can stand just anything."

Four paragraphs later, perhaps deceptively suggesting a rape has already occurred, she feels "her insides move in small, tickling clots, like loose shot." Other than that there is only the oblique moment of the rape: "Something is going to happen to me," then the scream "Something is happening to me!" and the fantasy of being outside at the old man's feet. That is all. Elsewhere instead of reflections we see Temple running, springing, crouching; see her moving distractedly in the room; hear her talk; see what she sees.

The narrative is lean, but that is hardly the word for the language. Stylistically there may be some debt to Hemingway as well as to detective fiction, but the greater affinity is with Flaubert. The strategy on the one hand is to juxtapose scenes of natural beauty with the sordid, the mean, the violent, by way of ironic commentary, and to maintain aesthetic distance. The corresponding strategy is to make precision and beauty of language, as it copes with meanness and depravity, function in the same way. Ideally the two strategies go hand in hand. They do in the humble event of Temple relieving herself outdoors. She moves through a lovely Mississippi landscape, but it is not lovely to her, who is almost as alien there as Popeye: the weeds *slash* at her. And the words *scar* and *sunshot,* for all their denotative precision, suggest a world full of menace. The turn of the next to last sentence is Flaubertian, with its denigrative *"kind of despair";* so too the sentence before that, with its placing of *clung* and its swift dying fall. We are, as often with Emma Bovary, both inside and out; see both Temple and the world she sees, as she stoops and twists "through a fence of sagging rusty wire and ran downhill among trees":

> At the bottom of the hill a narrow scar of sand divided the two slopes of a small valley, winding in a series of dazzling splotches where the sun found it. Temple stood in the sand, listening to the birds among the sunshot leaves, listening, looking about. She followed the dry runlet to where a jutting shoulder formed a nook matted with briers. Among the new green last year's dead leaves from the branches overhead clung, not yet fallen to earth. She stood here for a while, folding and folding the sheets in her fingers, in a kind of despair. When she rose she saw, upon the glittering mass of leaves along the crest of the ditch, the squatting outline of a man.

Two brief descriptions of Ruby's child combine Flaubert's coldness of clinical detail and composed "written" style with the distancing device of abrupt allusion to something very remote, here Paris street beggars. The two passages come some 20,000 words apart:

> Upon the lumpy wad of bedding it could be distinguished only by a series of pale shadows in soft small curves, and she went and stood over the box and looked down at its putty-colored face and bluish eyelids. A thin whisper of shadow cupped its head and lay moist upon its brow; one arm, upflung, lay curl-palmed beside its cheek.

> It lay in a sort of drugged immobility, like the children which beggars on Paris streets carry, its pinched face slick with faint moisture, its hair a damp whisper of shadow across its gaunt, veined skull, a thin crescent of white showing beneath its lead-colored eyelids.

The last sentence suggests, as Temple remarks after the earlier one, that this child is going to die. Flaubert too, recording the chatter of the shucks inside the mattress where Temple lay, might have seen "her hands crossed on her breast and her legs straight and close and decorous, like an effigy on an ancient tomb."

These remarks are not intended to suggest pastiche, but only to note affinities with the most conscious and controlled of stylists. It is pleasing to see a sentence begin with a Flaubertian notation of the Saturday countrymen in town, tranquil as sheep, move to an altogether Flaubertian yoking of cattle and gods, but end with Faulknerian sinuous rhythm and glamor:

> Slow as sheep they moved, tranquil, impassable, filling the passages, contemplating the fretful hurrying of those in urban shirts and collars with the large, mild inscrutability of cattle or of gods, functioning outside of time, having left time lying upon the slow and imponderable land green with corn and cotton in the yellow afternoon.

This is the crowd that, again leaving the land, will be back on Monday to visit the undertaker's parlor where Tommy lies dead.

A novel totally free from "Faulknerese" is inconceivable, and *Sanctuary* has its amusing instances. Temple's limited view of fading light in Memphis gives way, through a clock face, to "a disc suspended in nothingness" and ultimately to no less than "the ordered chaos of the intricate and shadowy world upon whose scarred flanks the old wounds whirl onward at dizzy speed into a darkness lurking with new disasters." He would be a purist indeed who begrudged such momentary extravagances. More regrettable is the highly literary consciousness and decadent rhetoric of Horace Benbow, some of which goes as far back as *Soldiers' Pay:* the view, for instance, of the college girls as "pagan and evanescent and serene, thinly evocative of all lost days and outpaced delights." Horace's preoccupations are inherited from an earlier version, where he played a more important part. His confrontation with Popeye at the spring is excellent, and his sardonic talk there persuasive. But his drunken monologue in the second chapter reads as though memorized from something he had published in a college literary magazine of the early twenties. "So each spring I could watch the reaffirmation of the old ferment hiding the hammock; the green-snared promise of unease. What blossoms grapes have, this is. It's not much: a wild and waxlike bleeding less of bloom than leaf, hiding and hiding the hammock." Such writing, and the implausibly remembered dialogue with Little Belle, initiate the misogynous vision. But its prettiness threatens to destroy the reality of the Old Frenchman Place. The decadent rhetoric has close affinities with Faulkner's early poems. Generally speaking, the educated consciousness in Faulkner is at a disadvantage—whether Benbow's, or Gavin Stevens's in other novels—as against the earthy or laconic talk of the blacks and Ratliff, and as against the raw reality of those who physically suffer and die, the criminals and their victims and the very poor.

Horace Benbow is in some ways useful to plot. The confrontation at the spring gives the novel a great start, and there are advantages to seeing the sinister Frenchman Place environment before Temple and Gowan get there. The novel depends on two coincidences—that Horace should leave the road for a drink at this particular spring, on his walk from Kinston, and that he should meet Clarence Snopes on the train. But these are meaningful enough in a fiction where the ordinary safe world and the hidden criminal society are seen to be so close. Clarence Snopes brilliantly exemplifies the knowing corrupt politician who moves at ease in both. Horace has his one effective moment of quick intelligence as a lawyer, when he resumes the conversation with Snopes. But Snopes's mind moves quicker still. Horace's education in evil, which has been stressed by some critics, is hardly essential to the novel, though his final surrender is a moving act of despair. He does not, like Temple and her father, go to Europe as he had dreamed of doing; his return to Belle, to the horror, is that of a man whose will has been broken. It is an important moment in the overall misogynous vision. Horace is not necessary, however, as an outside moral intelligence. For that moral intelligence, a very firm one, is supplied by controlling technique and controlled vision, and most obviously by evaluative style.

The essential fact of structure is the willed compression we have noted. The overall movement of the novel is remarkably firm, astonishingly so when we consider how much revision consisted of reshuffling chapters, with much pasting of galleys and rewriting. The introduction of Clarence Snopes, a fine comic rather than sinister portrait, brings new energy when it is needed. But even more important are the justly famous but rarely discussed chapters of Virgil and Fonzo at Miss Reba's (chap. 21) and of Red's funeral and its aftermath (chap. 25). Michael Millgate interestingly calls attention to similarities between *Sanctuary* and *Measure for Measure;* we might add that the Virgil/Fonzo episode is altogether Shakespearean, both in its sustained comedy and in the rhetorical effect of its coming at this juncture. In the simplest terms it may be said to bring comic relief and a necessary relief from tension. From the start and through chapter 24 and the report of a death at the Old Frenchman Place, over thirty thousand words, the taut narrative has commanded exceptional fixity of attention. There are no vacant places or instances of slack, neutral language to invite reader revery. Chapters 25–27, largely seen through Horace's eyes, return us to a more ordinary but depressing world. The long chapter 28, relieved only by Miss Reba and the snapping dogs, carries the still-bleeding Temple from the Old Frenchman Place to the bed on which she lies thrashing, with Popeye beside her bed making his high whinnying sound. In chapters 19 and 20, with Horace again, we contemplate his steadily darkening world, into which the fat obscene reality of Senator Clarence Snopes twice briefly intrudes. Chapter 20 ends with Snopes announcing he (who "if it's there" knows "where it is") is going to Memphis.

Instead, with chapter 21, it is Virgil Snopes we see arriving in Memphis, with Fonzo: the one pretending to know where things

are, the other on his first trip and eager for adventure. The great
chapter is so memorable that it is shocking to discover how short it
is, some three thousand words: the search for a hotel, and Fonzo's
growing awareness of his guide's ignorance, the hesitation before a
house with two fluffy white dogs in the yard, the discovery that Miss
Reba has daughters, the speculation that she must be a dressmaker
(since they have found a woman's undergarment under the wash-
stand), their visit to a brothel which must be kept secret from their
"landlady," and the appearance of cousin Clarence, who berates
them for their folly in spending three dollars on pleasure, when
cheaper negro establishments are available. The chapter, while
physically within the novel's world of depravity, has in fact freed us
from it into a purely aesthetic world of unalloyed joy, with disbelief
suspended. There is no lapse in the bright innocence and gullibility of
the two hicks, whose inferences are always wrong. The exchanges
are kept very brief, giving the reader no time to protest. No fools
outside Shakespeare are more innocent than the two returning from
the brothel, worried that Miss Reba will evict them. With Clarence's
appearance, and his sardonic comment at the negro whorehouse, we
return to a world in which evil and suffering are real. But for these
few pages, two-thirds through a dark experience, we have been
entirely freed from it, as we are in various Shakespearean interludes.

The relationship of real world and world of aesthetic play is,
with Red's funeral party, somewhat more complex. The chapter
complements and complicates the novel's darker intensities, rather
than freeing us from them entirely. The preceding chapter (chap. 24)
begins with Temple restless in her cage, demanding more to drink,
making what will prove a fatal telephone call. We see her in the car
with Popeye, with whom she is now on familiar terms: can call him
"daddy" yet pour out her scorn of his impotence, and be silenced by
his ringed hand, the ring "like a dentist's instrument." The scene at
the Grotto is intensely cinematographic: laconic dialogue, the music
and the dancers and the four sinister men; Red standing in the door;
the crap table and Temple's drunken gambling; her demand for a
room; the intense dialogue with Red, while her hips grind against
him. The brief paragraph of her writhing nymphomania is in a
normal novelistic mode. But the rest of the chapter keeps to the
cinematographic manner, and creates a world in which gangsters'
thugs may force one across a dance floor, and a man condemned to
death, perhaps knowing himself doomed, can raise his hand in "a

short, cheery salute." By the end of the chapter we are altogether in the world of the movies, a stylized world with its different kind of "reality."

The movement of chapter 24, both in timing and in detail, is thus from fairly conventional novelistic realism to the stylization of the gangster film, where death is not quite real. This movement prepares us for chapter 25's "atmosphere of macabre paradox," and the grotesque and parodic black humor of the funeral party. The initial shock (Red throwing dice, then on the next page in a coffin) is perhaps essential, by way of preparation for the fun, with the mourners as far from the real reality of death as Virgil and Fonzo from the reality of Miss Reba's. Our attention is recurringly fixed on the huge bowl of punch on the table draped in black, which will be a fulcrum for the steadily increasing disorder: "They surged and clamored about the diminishing bowl." But attention is also called to the bouncer, the "bullet-headed man who appeared to be on the point of bursting out of his dinner-jacket through the rear, like a cocoon." For it is he, the professional queller of disorder, who will ultimately bring on the catastrophe, and the corpse tumbling to the floor, the wreath coming too, "attached to him by a hidden end of a wire driven into his cheek." The outbreak of violence matches that of *The Day of the Locust*. But in this moment of chaos Faulkner's imagination anticipates the movement of Flem's spotted horses:

> The bouncer whirled again and met the rush of the four men. They mingled; a second man flew out and skittered along the floor on his back; the bouncer sprang free. Then he whirled and rushed them and in a whirling plunge they bore down upon the bier and crashed into it. The orchestra had ceased and were now climbing onto their chairs, with their instruments. The floral offerings flew; the coffin teetered. "Catch it!" a voice shouted. They sprang forward, but the coffin crashed heavily to the floor, coming open. The corpse tumbled slowly and sedately out and came to rest with its face in the center of a wreath.

As the novel has modulated through the stylization of cinema to this wild anti realist fun, so now it modulates back toward novelistic realism, and the darkness of Goodwin on trial. It must return from a parodic view of an outside world of anonymous strangers, the gangsters at the funeral party, to the very small world of Horace,

Goodwin, Ruby, ultimately Popeye and Temple. The modulation is accomplished brilliantly through a reprise of Miss Reba back at home after the party (the two snapping dogs flung back "against the wall in muted thuds"), drinking with Miss Myrtle and Miss Lorraine. At first the talk is playful, and death is still unreal; Red as a corpse "looked sweet." But gradually, as the women go on drinking, and as Miss Reba thinks of herself and Mr. Binford, two doves not two dogs, the talk turns professional, and to Red's folly in taking a chance with Popeye's girl. There is another joking exchange, but with an underlying seriousness: the respectable shooting gallery Miss Reba had run for thirty years, which Popeye tried to turn into a peep-show. The narrative becomes more serious, until Miss Reba at last evokes, for the first time very explicitly, the sexual triad: "Yes, sir, Minnie said the two of them would be nekkid as two snakes, and Popeye hanging over the foot of the bed without even his hat off, making a kind of whinnying sound."

These chapters, and *Sanctuary* generally, reveal much technical expertness and aesthetic tact in what should finally be regarded, like *The Secret Agent,* as a serious and even tragic *entertainment,* one based on a deliberately selective view of reality and an unashamedly misogynous vision. But to say this is not in the least to say that it is not a high work of art. And it is art—as we look back on the kindred challenges of personal obsession: on Dickens's revery in its sentimental extremes, on the great insight but also the disorder of Dostoevsky's—that makes the difference.

Sanctuary: The Persecuted Maiden, or, Vice Triumphant

Elizabeth M. Kerr

Sanctuary concludes both the story of the Sartoris family as active characters in Yoknapatawpha in the twentieth century and the story of Horace Benbow. (Narcissa and Aunt Jenny reappear in "There Was a Queen.") A Gothic theme is immediately suggested by the very title, *Sanctuary,* with its meaning of a refuge and an asylum: as Faulkner said at Nagano: "some safe secure place" to which a person can flee from trouble. In *The Achievement of William Faulkner,* Michael Millgate cited passages from *Measure for Measure* and Oscar Wilde's *Salome* as clues to the meaning of "sanctuary" and "temple." The meaning of "sanctuary" as a refuge for the criminal, as revealed in the end of Temple's story, is the clue to the ironic inversion which prevails throughout the novel, lending it another dimension as a bitter satire on society and social institutions. Dr. Lawrence Kubie noted the irony in the use of this title for "a tale in which there is no right of sanctuary, where neither impotence nor potency, neither the life of the defiant rebel nor that of the acquiescent conformist, where neither the free play of instinctual expression nor the life which is dominated by a restricting conscience, provides one with any escape from an ultimate state of doom and disaster." Not only does *Sanctuary* represent the conflict between good and evil, sharply contrasted by Gothic polarity of setting and characters, but it does so in a combination of the basic seduction story with the detective story which is one of the narrative patterns derived from the Gothic novel.

From *William Faulkner's Gothic Domain.* © 1979 by Kennikat Press Corp.

The irony begins with this choice of the detective story pattern, which is much more obvious in the published version than in the unpublished galleys; "the detective story," as Northrop Frye said in *The Secular Scripture,* "operates, for the most part, in a deeply conservative social area, where the emphasis is on reintegrating the existing order," rather than, as in *Sanctuary,* on exposing the iniquities of such an order.

Except for Leslie Fiedler, in *Love and Death in the American Novel,* critics have tended to recognize as Gothic only the more violent and macabre scenes in *Sanctuary,* rather than the entire pattern of inversions and the consequent force of the contrast they provide between idealism and reality. The nightmare quality in *Sanctuary,* one of the most obvious aspects of the Gothic, has been recognized and analyzed, without identifying the tradition to which the literature of nightmare belongs. Without recognizing Gothicism in general or other Gothic elements in *Sanctuary,* William Rossky stated precisely the basic nightmare effect of Gothic fiction: "Terror emanates . . . perhaps principally—from the dark vision of an irrational, nightmarish universe." Much of the reader's reaction is produced by "a technique of nightmare": "Repeatedly the narrative evokes moments of dreamlike horror typical especially of a certain kind of nightmare. The dreamer is caught in impotent terror, paralyzed, deeply frightened, trying, yet unable, to act or to scream." Rossky's description of the whole experience of *Sanctuary* is succinct and memorable: "a kind of long soundless scream." One is reminded of Edvard Munch's painting, "The Scream," which Giliane Morell cited as the visual image equivalent to Benjy's silent cries of helplessness.

Too many critics who apply "Gothic" to *Sanctuary* or any other modern American novel are unaware that Gothic has always been, as Frederick Garber explained, "an amalgam . . . which is in part a collective of other modes" and that "it is through this quality as a collective that the Gothic reaches out to fulfill its own radical form and statement." Mario Materassi saw *Sanctuary* as made up of three structures: the Gothic novel, in a modern world of delinquency and paranoia; the tall tale, in a bourgeois milieu; the tale of the antihero of the twentieth century, unable to cope with reality. The three structures are really a Gothic amalgam. Dealing with *Sanctuary* as a Gothic novel of horror, Douglas Perry analyzed it as representing the new American Gothic, defined by Irving Malin, with its "interaction of theme, image, and structure"; its themes of flight and confinement are "two sides of a coin," and narcissism is a third theme. Perry dealt also with three structural principles: *concentricity, predetermined sequence,* and *character repetition.* He explained that Faulkner, Capote, and Styron used the Gothic form "to capture the irony of our twentieth-century existence: the conviction that the search for self-awareness may not only be fatal, but fruitless, because it is equivalent to self-negation; that selfhood is an arbitrary construct of man's self-protective ignorance; that self-awareness and self-destruction are one and the same." Perry, in "Gothic as Vortex," did not relate "vortex" to "vorticism," which Donald Tritschler dealt with in "Whorls of Form in Faulkner's Fiction" (Ph.D. dissertation).

To the amalgam in *Sanctuary,* Pat Esslinger adds the influence of American comic strips and concludes: "Faulkner has indeed told an absorbing horror tale of prohibition days against the Gothic tapestry of his South, but he has also managed to embroider a magnificently grotesque thread of comic strip humor throughout his design." Joseph Blotner's account of the composition of *Sanctuary* indicates that Faulkner's character and the name "Popeye" were based on Popeye Pumphrey of Memphis and antedated the comic strip. But by the time Faulkner was writing *Sanctuary,* according to Thomas McHaney, the comic strip was new and may have influenced Faulkner's parodic development of Popeye. Esslinger points out that Horace and Popeye are doubles from the moment that their images are reflected in the pool: both are impotent, both lust after a girl to whom they bear a semipaternal relationship, and both meet their fate with resignation, defeat for Horace and death for Popeye. But unlike Faulkner's Popeye, Horace, like Popeye the Sailor Man, put a corncob to the innocent use of pipe-smoking.

More than any other novel by Faulkner, *Sanctuary* structurally emphasizes the "castles" and the "other rooms"; but the novel begins with an idyllic natural setting that ironically serves to stress the polarity of characters and places. The confrontation of Horace Benbow and Popeye at the spring, in which their images are reflected, anticipates their opposition as hero and villain in the detective story plot, and differentiates natural and unnatural man, Horace at ease in this sylvan setting and Popeye terrified by a bird in flight. In picturing Popeye Faulkner carried to an extreme Charles Dickens's device of dehumanizing description which turns people into things. Traditionally, the good guy, the detective, should win, and the bad guy, the criminal, should lose in the conflict between them, and the success of the detective should represent a reassuring triumph of justice. The action of *Sanctuary* takes place in spring and summer, and the outdoor scenes in Temple's story are chiefly sunny. The most extensive and ironic use of natural setting occurs in the trip of Popeye and Temple to Memphis: the "unbelievable soft radiance of May" in that "lavender spring" not only is the background of the violated Temple's flight with her grotesque captor but also suggests that the action is both a modern abduction of Persephone by Pluto and an inversion of fertility rites. In both T. S. Eliot's *The Waste Land* and Sir James G. Frazer's *The Golden Bough* Thomas McHaney found parallels to scenes, plot, and characters in *Sanctuary*.

The lack of fertility is apparent in the first view of the "haunted castle": "The house was a gutted ruin rising gaunt and stark out of a grove of unpruned cedar trees." On the sunny afternoon when Temple and Gowan first saw it, "nowhere was any sign of husbandry—plow or tool; in no direction was a planted field in sight." Edward Corridori remarked [in his Ph.D. dissertation] on the fashion in which, in a "realistic presentation of a locale," the description may "tend toward the irrational or unreal, or, perhaps, even the surreal," terms which fit the ruined mansion and its motley crew of inmates.

In its origin the Old Frenchman Place is comparable with Sutpen's Hundred or the Sartoris plantation: it was founded by Louis Grenier, who "was granted the first big land patent" and "brought the first slaves into the country" (*Requiem for a Nun*). The house appears in Yoknapatawpha fiction only as a ruin, never in either splendor or mere shabbiness. It is not only a ruin but also the scene of evil, formerly the scene of treasure hunts by those greedy for gold and now the hangout of bootleggers and gangsters. Warren Beck referred in *Faulkner* to "the Gothic and sordid ménage at Frenchman's Bend," and described *Sanctuary* as one of Faulkner's "most authentically regional novels." Jean Mayoux described Frenchman's Bend as sinister and mysterious, with "an atmosphere of incoherent sorcery, of alcoholic delirium." It represents a sanctuary for lawless invaders of the county, as Sartoris, home of established aristocrats, represents a sanctuary for a homecoming native son: the two houses continue the polarity established at the spring. The technique is Dickensian, resembling the use of locales in *Bleak House,* as William Axton observed, to "discriminate between the moral qualities associated with two circles of characters," the qualities of "transience and disorder" and "permanence and order." In *Sartoris,* however, permanence and order depend on Aunt Jenny, ninety years old and confined to a wheelchair. The shift of scene to the city, Memphis, continues the polarity of setting and adds another kind of Gothic scene outside of Yoknapatawpha County. Not only did Dickens use the city as the Gothic milieu of his most evil characters and darkest deeds, but to the writers of the Romantic decadence, George Gibian reported, the city was "attractive and evil; . . . beautiful and grotesque." The completely un-Dickensian defeat of virtue in *Sanctuary* is the more impressive when the similarity to Dickensian Gothic techniques is noted.

The third mansion, Miss Reba's in Memphis, Dickens would not have dared to introduce into his novels, read aloud in the family circle, but it belongs to the Gothic tradition, brothels being not uncommon scenes. The appearance of respectability which Miss Reba maintains in her "sanctuary" is less ironic than that which Narcissa Benbow Sartoris preserved at the cost of an innocent man's life. Obviously, a brothel is a place of entrapment or imprisonment, prominent among the scenes of enclosure in *Sanctuary*. These scenes contribute, William Rossky said, to "the sense of cold paralysis, entrapment and terror which permeates *Sanctuary* and becomes a feeling about existence itself." The use of the three houses—the Old Frenchman Place, Sartoris, and Miss Reba's—with Horace as the connecting character, offers a parallel to Dickens's *Great Expectations,* in which "literal landmarks," as Taylor Stoehr observed are "landmarks of structure" as in dreams, and "place has an organizing function beyond that of mere background."

In these houses and other buildings scenes of enclosure or imprisonment are used with maximum frequency and effectiveness. In the Old Frenchman Place there is a climactic succession in Temple's search for sanctuary, from the kitchen where she was safe with Ruby, to the room where she spent the night, physically unharmed, to the barn, and finally to the crib, a suitably ambiguous term. The facts that Miss Reba's is a crib in one sense and that the Grotto, the nightclub in Memphis, suggests ancient nativity scenes in a grotto establish a manger-crib association which seems further evidence of the ironic intention. Temple's room in Miss Reba's is both the scene of her imprisonment and of Popeye's voyeurism, and the scene of her confrontation with Horace, thus serving in both the seduction and the detection plots. Horace's room at Sartoris is the scene of a parallel confrontation with Narcissa which leads to her visit to the district attorney and the consequent defeat of Horace. Temple's successive refuges are paralleled, as Olga Vickery observed, by the successive scenes of literal sanctuary for Ruby—Horace's house, the hotel, the shack of the crazy woman, and the jail—but, unlike Temple, Ruby cannot save herself by flight and suffers increasing deprivation in trying to save Lee. The jail, the most obvious scene of imprisonment, ironically is a sanctuary more fully than the other refuges: Lee Goodwin was safe from Popeye when he was in jail. After the first day of the trial, Horace and Ruby shared the cell with Lee. The courtroom, the last scene of enclosure, shares with jails and prisons a long history in the Gothic novel. Devendra Varma credited Anne Radcliffe with the first use of a courtroom in a Gothic novel. In *The Secular Scripture,* Northrop Frye traced courtroom scenes to romance, in which an unjust trial was common near the end. The unjust trial in *Sanctuary* introduced the court scenes which became recurrent in Faulkner's fiction. After the trial, Lee was violently taken from the sanctuary of the jail and was lynched. Both outdoor and interior scenes in *Sanctuary* are used dramatically for contrasts between characters, for ironic contrasts between natural setting and action, and for a sense of imprisonment which may be literal with Lee and Ruby, or psychological with Temple.

Temple, a modern version of the Persecuted Maiden, most obviously represents Faulkner's inversion of characters who belong to familiar types. The strongly allegorical aspects of *Sanctuary* are suggested by some of the names. Leslie Fiedler noted in *Love and Death* that " 'Temple Drake' evokes both a ruined sanctuary and the sense of an unnatural usurpation: woman become a sexual aggressor—more drake than duck." By her disobedience in going with Gowan and her refusal to leave the Old Frenchman Place, Temple initiated and stimulated the events leading to her rape. The nightmare effect is so overwhelming that the reader may overlook her lack of serious effort to save herself, but her admission in *Requiem for a Nun* that she could have escaped at any time after Gowan wrecked the car confirms what the astute reader could detect through the inversion of the Gothic pattern in the character of Temple and the pattern of action. Mary D. Fletcher [in her Ph.D. dissertation] regarded Temple as illustrating an implicitly Calvinistic view of man as "a depraved creature who yearns not toward good but toward evil."

Dr. Lawrence Kubie summed up Temple's behavior and the irony of the consequences:

> It is the uttermost limits of sour irony that this impudent, tantalizing, and provocative young girl, who had played fast and loose with the men of her own world without ever giving them the gift she kept dangling in front of them, should escape the relatively honest erotic purposes of the healthy members of the band, only to taunt the impotent and tortured figure of Popeye into committing a criminal assault upon her by artificial means.

Temple is narcissistic; her compact and mirror provide repeated reflection images, most significantly when she carefully powders and preens before lying down with the expectation of being raped and before going to the Grotto with Popeye. Artificial to the point of being unnatural, with a masklike face, Temple illustrates Horace Benbow's analogy between the mirror, symbolizing Progress, and the grape arbor, symbolizing Nature: Temple and Little Belle show the same kind of dissimulation and absorption in self. That they are doubles is revealed explicitly in Horace's nauseating vision of them merged in a surrealistic image suggesting the heroine of melodrama or early motion pictures, tied to a railroad track.

In appearance Temple is the Flapper Temptress: "arrowlike in her scant dress" she suggested a hermaphrodite figure to Joachim Seyppel. Narcissa, a widow, was still dressed in white for her role of the Pure White Virgin. In *The Secular Scripture,* Northrop Frye cited the use in romance of "the device of the doubled heroine, sometimes represented by a dark and a fair girl, sometimes linked to a grave-and-gay contrast of temperament." Narcissa had dark hair and "a broad, stupid, serene face"; Temple had red hair. At the trial, Temple switched roles, from the Flapper Temptress to the Persecuted Maiden, in her Violated Virgin Phase. Both Temple and Narcissa are sources of evil, overt in Temple except in the courtroom and covert in Narcissa. In *Sanctuary* Narcissa revealed how deceptive she was in appearance. She had no moral scruples, and, putting respectability above justice, she ruthlessly caused the defeat of Horace in his first serious and crucial professional case and callously sacrificed the life of Lee Goodwin. Within her own social context Miss Reba, the madam of a brothel, was motivated by the same desire as Narcissa, that of maintaining a respectable house. Grotesque as she was, Miss Reba had capacity for love and compassion and, by comparison with Narcissa's mindless serenity, was a sympathetic character instead of the traditional Evil Woman, the prostitute.

Ruby Lamar, another Evil Woman in her identity as a former prostitute and an unmarried mother, was really the Suffering Wife. Her name combines that of L. Q. C. Lamar, Oxford's most distinguished citizen before William Faulkner, with, perhaps, an allusion to the virtuous woman in Proverbs whose "price is far above rubies." Although Ruby would sacrifice her "virtue" to save Lee, Narcissa would sacrifice nothing for anyone but herself: to save her image unblemished in the public eye, Narcissa offered herself to the FBI man, in return for the mash notes of Byron Snopes, and was accepted ("There Was a Queen"). But she hounded Ruby from one refuge to another because Ruby and Lee were not married. The complete inversion in Temple and Narcissa of traditional roles is confirmed in the other works in which they appear, Temple in *Requiem for a Nun* and Narcissa in *Sartoris-Flags in the Dust* and "There Was a Queen." To some extent this inversion remains true also of Miss Reba: in *The Reivers* she reappears in her Memphis establishment but plays a completely sympathetic and highly amusing role.

Because Aunt Jenny's virtue was genuine and she scorned conventional appearances, she is never presented ironically. In "An Odor of Verbena," *Sartoris, Sanctuary,* and "There Was a Queen" she was devoid of phony gentility and sentimental romanticism. To Narcissa's wail about Horace bringing "a street walker, a murderess" into the Benbow house, Aunt Jenny retorted scornfully, "Fiddle-sticks."

Except for Popeye as the villain, the other male characters show consistent inversion of traditional roles. Gowan Stevens is a parody of the Romantic hero; he judged a gentleman only by the way he held his liquor and, by his own standards, was no gentleman. Having chosen the role of the champion and protector of Temple, Gowan ran away and left her as soon as he was sober enough to leave the Old Frenchman Place, much as Bayard Sartoris ran away when he had caused his grandfather's death. Red, Gowan's successor as Temple's champion, was much more to her taste than Gowan. Red also was cast in a hero's role and was unable to play the part. Less craven than Gowan, Red at least died as a victim instead of running away. According to tradition in either Gothic or detective fiction,

Horace Benbow, the lawyer-detective, should win his case and secure the triumph of virtue over vice. But he is an idealistic hero quixotically accepting a challenge, rather than a criminal lawyer able to use the information he gathered to win the case for his innocent client. His moral courage proved ineffective when he faced collusion between the guilty ones and the other lawyers. He discovered that his society, like that described by Frye in *The Secular Scripture,* wished "to remain in a blind and gigantic darkness" in which he saw no light.

Horace's own weakness defeated him: his incestuous love for Narcissa and his adulterous and then marital love for Belle made him their victim. The romantic naiveté he showed in *Sartoris* is evident also in *Sanctuary*. (In both *Flags in the Dust* and the unpublished galleys of *Sanctuary,* Horace showed much greater self-knowledge.) In *Sanctuary* the incestuous nature of his love for Little Belle, his stepdaughter, was one of the shattering revelations he experienced in his belated initiation, at the age of forty-three, into the reality of adult life. Olga Vickery saw Popeye and Horace as polar opposites, Popeye, the villain, being "isolated by his total indifference to all moral values" and Horace, the hero, being "isolated by his dream of moral perfection." Popeye could act but not feel; Horace could feel but not act effectively. Horace is not an ironic inversion of the romantic hero; the irony lies in his inability to play the role he unselfishly chose. That he was totally unprepared for that role is clear in *Flags in the Dust* and is implied in *Sartoris*. Horace was like a man who jumped into the water to save a drowning man without being able to swim.

The only virile male character in *Sanctuary,* Lee Goodwin should be a villain: neither heroic nor respectable, he was a disreputable bootlegger engaged in no more hazardous traffic than bringing contraband liquor into Yoknapatawpha and selling it to the leading citizens. But Lee is an ironic inversion precisely as Ruby is: his name, "Lee," is that of the greatest southern hero, and "Goodwin," which means "friend of god," may also be read as Good Win, signifying the hero's triumph. As the victim, convicted of crimes of which he was innocent, and as the scapegoat who suffered a horrible death, Lee is more nearly a hero than Horace. Lee resembles the romance hero, subjected to an unjust trial, but unlike such heroes as described by Northrop Frye, Lee had "no vision of liberation." Lee tried to keep the invaders of his sanctuary from being harmed. Guilty of homicidal violence in the past, Lee was innocent of violence in *Sanctuary*. Like Marlow in *Heart of Darkness*, Lee chose his nightmare: to take sanctuary in the jail and trust that Horace could win the trial of an innocent man, rather than to inform against Popeye and be shot by him.

Popeye seems to be the only male character who does not represent an inversion of a traditional role: he is unmistakably a villain, twice a murderer in the novel. In addition, he is a sadist, a rapist, and an impotent voyeur. Leslie Fiedler in *Love and Death* described Popeye as "the most revolting avatar of the desexed seducer" and "a terrible caricature of the child witness," as he watched Red and Temple. The ugliness of this perversion is obvious, but as Olga Vickery observed, it is paralleled by "Horace's painful exclusion from the grape arbor where Little Belle casually experiments with sex." Popeye's violence is akin to Horace's "fantasy and hallucination"; "Popeye's brutal act fuses with Horace's thoughts and culminates in the nightmare vision of the rape of a composite Temple-Little Belle." Popeye's physical grotesqueness and his psychological abnormalities being caused by hereditary disease, he is not a villain in the Gothic sense of a self-willed evildoer. William Brown [in his Ph.D. dissertation] considered Popeye a sociopath, so closely fitting definitions of sociopathy that he was convinced that Faulkner "drew deliberately from such professional material in the creation of the characters." In other respects than as victim and violator, Temple and Popeye are doubles. In "Faulkner's Paradox in Pathology and Salvation," William Brown noted that both are "repeatedly described as 'doll-like,' " Temple "in the slang sense of a pretty but dumb girl" and Popeye "in the sense of a puppet. . . . He is a puppet physically and psychologically in that he is moved by a constitutional deformity rather than by a free mind." Jean Mayoux commented on Temple and Popeye as being grotesque in their motions, like puppets, and as showing dissociation of mind and body in a state of tension. He commented also on the effect of strangeness Faulkner created by oddity in physiognomy and on the dreamlike quality of *Sanctuary*.

The closest straight parallel to a traditional Gothic type seems to be Judge Drake, who resembles the Tyrannical Father, with a double in Ruby's father, who shot Frank. But Judge Drake's tyranny, so far as one can tell, consisted in his attempts to protect his daughter, first by laying down rules of conduct and then by making her save her reputation by perjury and the consequent miscarriage of justice. The implication of the tableau of Temple's reluctant exit from court is that Judge Drake and her four brothers used pressure to keep her from besmirching the family name by testifying truthfully. Thus, tyranny takes a new form and the judge subverts justice.

In addition to Popeye, wholly grotesque, and the grotesque aspects and un-Dickensian perversion of the characters already discussed, *Sanctuary* exhibits a larger number of minor Dickensian grotesques than any other of Faulkner's Gothic novels. Northrop Frye, in *A Study of English Romanticism,* traced back to medieval and Renaissance courts the custom, imitated in romance, of utilizing "fools, dwarfs, and cripples . . . to serve the purpose of *memento mori.*" (Horace thought that Popeye, diminutive if not a dwarf, smelled black, "like that black stuff that ran out of Bovary's mouth.") With uncanny aptness in relation to *Sanctuary,* Frye referred to the grotesque in literature as "the expression . . . of the nauseated vision." Tommy, the humorous servant, was too simple and innocent to fear Popeye and was killed for trying to protect Temple, in the hope that she would keep her promise to him. The blind man at the Old Frenchman Place, hands on stick, has a double at the end in Judge Drake, in the same posture, with the obvious implication of another kind of blindness. That the blind man is not merely a gratuitous horror is further made evident in the way in which, as William Rossky said, he "contributes to the sense of universal nightmare," "epitomizes . . . the horror of human decay . . . becomes man as impotent victim of the cosmic condition." He is like the blind beggar who haunted Emma Bovary. Horace's allusion to "Bovary" confirms Rossky's comparison. At the other end of human life is Ruby's baby, pathetically grotesque with its "putty-colored face and bluish eyelids."

The repulsive Clarence Snopes, the keyhole voyeur, had a putty-like, flabby face and the nose of some "weak, acquisitive creature like a squirrel or a rat." The physical deformity of Eustace Graham, the crippled district attorney, reflected his warped morals; his "clumsy clog-step" and finger snapping celebrated his gaining the knowledge that would serve his personal ends and cause the death of Lee Goodwin. Miss Reba, obese, wheezy, and oddly clad, accompanied by her "white, worm-like dogs," is an unforgettable Dickensian grotesque in appearance and speech, if not in profession. The innocence of the country bumpkins Virgil and Fonzo, who mistook Miss Reba's for a boarding house for girls and took their patronage elsewhere, serves as a contrast to the full awareness of Temple, no older than they, of the nature of the house. Dickensian burlesque with an un-Dickensian setting is also evident in the episode of Miss Reba and her decorous lady friends, mentors of the inebriated six-year-old Uncle Bud. These grotesque characters and situations visibly represent a corrupt society and its distorted values. William Rossky saw in Miss Reba's poodles a comment "on the behavior of men within the nightmare world of the novel . . . vicious, snarling and even mad in their relationship." Describing the structural principle of concentricity as like a vortex, with a series of events funneling into a final one, Douglas Perry remarked that at successive levels the main characters become more grotesque.

The two basic patterns of the action which takes place in this society, with this cast of characters, are both inverted: the seduction of Temple who refused to flee and the successful but unavailing detective search by Horace which served as a belated initiation into an adult reality too harsh for him to live in. The nightmare-dream pattern predominates in the subjective passages, which center in Temple and Horace. The alternation between these two central figures is so handled as to heighten mystery and suspense. The most traditional suspense is the delayed rape at the Old Frenchman Place, a pattern which originated in Richardson's *Clarissa Harlowe*. The abrupt break after Tommy is shot is the means by which the mystery of just what did happen to Temple can be maintained until near the end of the trial. The detective story raises the usual questions: Will Horace discover the truth? Will he succeed in the trial? The obscurity of the motives of those opposed to Horace, especially the connection between Judge Drake and Popeye in concealing the truth, is due largely to the omission of details about the period between Horace's interview with Temple and the trial; Faulkner was deliberately heightening the Gothic effect.

The mysteries of Clarence Snopes's dealings with Judge Drake and the Memphis lawyer somewhat overshadow the central question: Will Temple testify to the truth? The structure, placing the court scenes very near the end, makes the revelation of the answer dramatically effective. The horrible death of Lee Goodwin diverts the reader's attention from the question which remains: Why did Temple commit perjury and cause the death of Lee Goodwin for a crime he did not commit? Dr. Kubie suggests an answer that is consistent with what happens to the virile men in the book and that might be extended from

Temple and her hatred of her father and brothers to other respectable women in society: " 'To be a woman is worse than death or the same as death. Therefore I will take my revenge upon all you men who are really men. . . . And finally I will be the instrument of your actual bodily destruction.' " Kubie may be right in explaining Temple's motive as revenge, a Gothic theme which Faulkner used subtly in Miss Rosa's revenge on Sutpen. Since it was Lee who suffered, Temple may have sought revenge on him because he did not respond to her coquetry, by which she invited the fate she feared.

Gothic fiction can offer few examples of the girl-in-flight pattern in which motion is so prominent in incident and imagery as in *Sanctuary*. As Leslie Fiedler said in *Love and Death,* "Faulkner's Temple figures are sheer motion, a blur of dancing legs and wind-blown hair in a speeding car." Most significant are the scenes where she is running, even running into space "right off the porch, into the weeds." But the flight that traditionally should save virtue is for Temple erratic and circular and is succeeded by passive captivity. The flight began when she got off the train to ride with Gowan, a flight from her father's instructions and the university rules, a flight from respectability and conventional morality. At the Old Frenchman Place she refused to flee when Ruby advised her to. Temple's flights in and around the house were more provocative than elusive. As Olga Vickery explained, she never can make up her mind to take effective flight: "It is not her fear of encountering greater evils or dangers but her fascination with the idea of violence that holds her immobile." Even attempts at flight ceased when she left with Popeye. At Miss Reba's she merely played "the role of 'victim-prisoner,' " as Olga Vickery said, having abandoned "all the social values of her group without accepting the personal values which, however minimal, lend significance to the lives of Ruby and Goodwin." Faulkner confirmed this interpretation in *Requiem for a Nun,* where Temple confessed that she stayed at Miss Reba's because she was corrupt. For physical flight Temple substituted flight from reality in the fantasies she related to Horace, which add to the theme of sexuality and sexual perversion. Dr. Kubie explained that the fantasy of change of sex and her

> rude awakening from this dream . . . gave rise to a secondary phantasy (one which is familiar enough to psychoanalysts in their study of illness, but rarely encoun-

tered in literature), in which there was a fusion of the ideas of rape, castration, and death. . . . From that moment Temple behaves as though she herself were dead, and the blind, dead instrument of revenge.

Temple's story led up to Horace's surrealistic and nauseating image of Temple-Little Belle. After Temple was rescued by her father and brothers, who could have rescued her much earlier if she had told Miss Reba how to reach them, she fled again, with her father, to France. Although the image of the girl in flight remains shockingly vivid, the moral significance lies in the facts that she did not actually flee to save her virtue and that she protected her violator and brought death to Lee, her protector.

As the image of Temple is flight, that of Horace is quest. But Horace began by fleeing from Belle and reality, so suddenly that he took no money with him. But when he learned of the plight of Lee Goodwin, Horace yielded to his quixotic impulses and began his purposeful journeys. Horace's physical journeys in "strenuous quest for evidence," as Warren Beck said, took him back and forth from Sartoris to Jefferson, from Jefferson to Oxford, and from Jefferson to Memphis. His journey from Sartoris to Jefferson to reside in his own house was part of his choice to struggle for justice. His short journeys in behalf of Ruby, to find lodgings for her, and to the jail, to confer with Lee, provide much of the essential action and continuity.

His quest for truth and justice is also an initiation into the nature of evil and into the reality beneath social conduct and institutions. "In nearly every one of Faulkner's novels," as Cleanth Brooks said, in "Faulkner's *Sanctuary*," "the male's discovery of evil and reality is bound up with his discovery of the true nature of woman. Men idealize and romanticize women, but the cream of the jest is that women have a secret rapport with evil which men do not have, that they are able to adjust to evil without being shattered by it."

In this view of women the ironic inversion of the traditional Gothic novel is particularly obvious and significant. Brooks refers to Narcissa's shocking depravity, but he does not mention that the conventional Evil Women, Ruby and Reba, show no such depravity and do not shock Horace, except when Ruby revealed the evil in men: " 'Good God,' he whispered. 'What kind of men have you known?' " The irony in Horace's quest and initiation is that he is a lawyer forty-three years old who has never before seriously assumed his professional and social responsibilities. Heinrich Straumann charged Horace with both his inadequacy as a counsel and his capitulation, not stoic acceptance, after losing the case. Having suffered defeat in his first defense of a legally innocent man, he fled from evil and corruption and left them to flourish without his further opposition. His lack of experience as a lawyer is even more apparent in *Flags in the Dust,* where the nature of his law practice is specified, than in *Sartoris,* where his chief activities were glassblowing and being seduced by Belle Mitchell.

The shock of cognition and the fall from innocence, as Frederick Garber pointed out, were characteristic of the Gothic novel and of emerging Romanticism. In *Sanctuary* the shock and the fall are experienced by a middle-aged lawyer in his native town. *Sanctuary* stops short of "the full Gothic plot," which, Garber said, "moves from an initial confrontation to a fall into self-consciousness and then . . . to a phase of coping or learning to cope." (Horace's incorrigible inability to cope may have been one reason that Faulkner permanently consigned him to Kinston and never let him reenter Yoknapatawpha.) Horace's moral enlightenment, that "there's a corruption about even looking upon evil," gave rise to his vision "of a world left stark and dying above the tide-edge of the fluid in which it lived and breathed," "a motionless ball in cooling space, across which a thick smell of honeysuckle writhed like cold smoke." Gothic fiction has few such desperate images of apocalyptic annihilation, evoked by awareness of man's sexual nature, symbolized for Horace as for Quentin Compson by the smell of honeysuckle. The moonlight scene which is the context of the quotation, preceding the surrealistic Temple-Little Belle vision, adds a new dimension to romantic moonlight as a "prop" in Gothic fiction. With no reference to the Gothic tradition Olga Vickery's explanation of Horace's reaction precisely fits the reactions which produced some of the first Gothic novels: "What reduces Horace to a state of shock is the discovery not of evil but of the shoddy foundations of his vision of a moral and rational universe, supported and sustained by the institutions of the church, the state, and the law." The degree and nature of Narcissa's betrayal of him Horace seemed not to realize; his romantic idealism and lack of self-knowledge had helped him to make Narcissa what she was. In the revisions of both *Flags in the Dust* and *Sanctuary,* Horace's similar idealization and "innocence" had concealed from him his feeling for Little Belle. His initiation involved the loss of innocence and the acceptance of guilt, personal and social. All he could do about his new maturity was to flee back to Belle and the life he had found intolerable and lock the back door, knowing that Little Belle was at a houseparty.

As the unsuccessful but sympathetically portrayed hero, the impotent Horace most fully conveys the basic theme of the impotence of modern man and his "three direct objects of fear," as dramatized, according to Dr. Kubie, in *Sanctuary:* "a fear of women, a fear of other men, and a fear of the community and of society in general." If "heterosexual" is put in place of "other," the statement is remarkably close to the thesis of Leslie Fiedler's *Love and Death in the American Novel.* Dr. Kubie noted the destruction in *Sanctuary* of the only natural, vital, and potent males, Lee Goodwin, Red, and the Negro murderer in the jail, and explained the ironic significance of Popeye: "Popeye's very figure . . . is concretely described . . . in words which make it a graphic representation of the phallus whose impotence is the root of the whole tragedy."

In addition to the flight of Temple and her father from reality and notoriety, the last chapter presents Popeye's flight from justice. Here the facts of his earlier life, with the ironic birthdate of December 25 and with details of Gothic horror, indicate that he was not responsible for the course his life had taken. By application of diagnostic criteria to the account of Popeye, in "Faulkner's Paradox" William Brown concluded that Popeye represented "pathology . . . of a specific type recognized by psychiatrists" and that in Popeye Faulkner "undoubtedly creates a constitutional abnormality." Until Popeye left Memphis, where his influence provided him with safety from the law, his flight had been more figurative than literal. After the murder of Red, Popeye started "on his way to Pensacola to visit his mother" and was arrested en route and charged with a murder committed at the time of Red's murder. He made no attempt to defend himself. Popeye's own trial provided what Douglas Perry called "the final gothic twist, the final concentric pattern." Thus the ultimate irony is his acceptance of the death he had avoided by destroying Lee Goodwin. Popeye's last request before execution, "Fix my hair, Jack," adds a grotesque detail which Joanne Creighton described as the final "macabre caricature" of concern for social appearances, forms, and rituals.

The execution which follows is covered in three words: "springing the trap." The prevalence of the grotesque in characters and scenes, and the scenes of horror and violence produce in *Sanctuary* the authentic Gothic shudder. But mere sensationalism Faulkner often avoided by distancing or understating the violence, rather than elaborating upon it.

The most Gothic sequence of action, in mood and setting and incidents, occurs at the Old Frenchman Place. The ruined mansion, surrounded by desolation, and the sinister characters show the possibilities of Gothic effect from naturalistic details. The shift to subjective rendering, largely from Temple's point of view but including Tommy's and Ruby's, builds up the nightmare effect. But even here the switch to Temple's point of view omits some of the terror of the reality, as Temple's account to Horace revealed. The climax in the crib, with Temple like the cornered rat which terrifies her, stops short of the rape. The murder of Tommy is represented only by a sound "no louder than the striking of a match," the rape, only by Temple's silent scream to the old blind man, "Something is happening to me!"

What happened, but not how, is revealed in the account of the flight to Memphis; the beauty of the countryside is in ironic contrast to Temple's distress, which seems less than one might expect from similar experiences of the virtuous Clarissas of fiction. Temple's violation had been only physical, not moral. Despite the circumstances, speed is not stressed in Popeye's flight from the Old Frenchman Place.

The room at Miss Reba's symbolizes Temple's corruption. The details of the furnishings, especially the mirrors and the one-handed china clock with its four nymphs, and the descriptions of Temple's new possessions, particularly the platinum bag with orange banknotes in it, are modernized Gothic. The most extreme example of perverted sexuality, that of Red and Temple with Popeye as voyeur, shocked even Miss Reba, "him trying to turn" her respectable house "into a peep show." Dr. Kubie explained Popeye's voyeurism as an acting out of "the primitive horror-ridden phantasy" of the male who "is struggling with impotence fears": "the fantasy [sic] of being helpless and bound while someone else rapes the woman he loves." More within the range of normal sexuality but with a Southern "lady" as the aggressor is the scene between Temple and Red in which danger and lust are climactically mingled and Temple's eroticism is dramatically portrayed: as Fiedler said in *Love and Death,* "Not content to be violated, the woman becomes the violator," "whimpering for the consummation she had once fled in terror." (The terror, however, had been less powerful than the fascination.) The murder of Red, after this scene, is an anticlimax; it is suggested only by Popeye's "match flipped outward like a dying star in miniature," recalling the match that was the token of Tommy's murder.

The funeral of Red, discussed by David Frazier as an isolated Gothic scene, is most easily and convincingly explained as part of a Gothic novel, in which the macabre and grotesque details are completely appropriate. The whole ritual follows the pattern of a black mass, as William Stein demonstrated, even to the woman in red as the Whore of Babylon. The climax occurs when the corpse of Red tumbles out of the coffin and the bullet hole in its forehead is revealed. Grotesque incongruity follows: the social gathering at Miss Reba's, a parody of the decorum and respectability of the women of Jefferson, especially Narcissa, suggests that Miss Reba and her friends, grotesque as they seem, show more real feeling and sympathy than Narcissa would.

The last sequence of events, beginning with the trial, includes the quiet tension of the night Horace spent in the jail with Lee and Ruby, when he learned more about the kind of men Ruby had known and how she would have paid debts to them and about how his sheltered life looked to those who were familiar with vice and violence. On the next day of the trial, the horror of the rape is finally disclosed. The discovery and reversal occur when Temple perjures herself and Horace therefore faces defeat: he has learned the nature of reality beneath social conventions. The tableau of Temple forced out of court, surrounded by her father and four brothers, epitomizes the myth which is destroyed by the reality but preserved in appearance: the Pure Woman who has been protected by Southern Manhood with the aid of society and the legal system is in reality the cause of two murders and a lynching, as well as of her own corruption.

In addition to the scene between Temple and Red, the other scene in *Sanctuary* which receives the full Gothic treatment is what Douglas Perry called "the fiery vortex which engulfs Lee Goodwin," as witnessed by Horace who narrowly escaped Lee's fate. As William Rossky said: "The bonfire becomes the mesmerizing conflagration at the heart of everything"; "as in nightmare, the scene builds an effect of stasis in which powerlessness and enormous dread fuse." But the agonizing scene is cut short by Horace's lapse into unconsciousness.

Lee Goodwin was completely innocent of the murder of Tommy and the rape, as Temple knew. Misreading of *Sanctuary*, such as George Marion O'Donnell's, which attaches any validity to the case presented by the district attorney, deliberately framed according to the myth of the White Virgin inherited from courtly love and Southern Calvinism, completely misses the whole point for which Faulkner adapted the Gothic pattern. O'Donnell described Temple as "Southern Womanhood Corrupted but Undefiled" and asserted that even when she was "hopelessly corrupted by Modern Man," she was not the cause of Lee's death. That was what O'Donnell expected to read. But by careful and virtually complete inversion of both the story of seduction and the detective story, Faulkner used the Gothic tradition much as Dickens used comparable theatrical materials, as William Axton explained, "to arouse his readers' expectations that a realistic contemporary novel will imitate an ideal mythic action and then to frustrate or disorient these expectations by departure from, inversions of, and incongruous survivals" of original motifs. The contrast between appearance and reality is sharpened by the traditional roles in which characters seem to be cast but which, when they play their parts, reveal dramatically how the forces inherent in respectable Southern society have created a false image of Southern womanhood and false moral views, and how justice is subverted to preserve that image and those views.

Dr. Lawrence Kubie interpreted *Sanctuary* as a dramatization of the struggle "between the forces of instinctual evil" and "the forces of an evil and savage conscience, operating through the blind vengefulness of a misdirected mob." Horace is "the weak representative of the much-battered 'Ego,' that fragment of the personality which is so often ground to pieces in the battle." The inclusion of Horace and Narcissa extends the relevance of the story beyond the story of Temple, a flapper of the twenties from Jackson. Horace and Narcissa, not having responded to the spirit of the flapper age, represent the values Temple rejected; their previous rules identify them as representing the natives of Jefferson. Thus, the attempt to secure justice and the successful action to defeat it are rooted in the community and its traditions, represented not only by the Benbows but also by the Snopeses and Eustace Graham, who were introduced in *Sartoris*. By omission of racial complications in the sexual theme,

Faulkner avoided inclusion of an element so highly charged emotionally that it might obscure his inversion of characters and values.

Like *Sartoris* and *Absalom, Absalom!* the published version of *Sanctuary* differs from an earlier version and comparison of the two is pertinent to Gothic elements in the final version. In *Faulkner's Revision of "Sanctuary": A Collation of the Unrevised Galleys and the Published Book,* Gerald Langford made available the passages in the galleys which were altered or omitted in the book and showed the extensive structural changes effected through excision and rearrangement. Langford did not perceive that Gothic patterns and the detective quest-initiation are basic to the revision, in which characters, settings, and dramatic conflict are polarized.

The material from the galleys shows that Gothic elements were retained or strengthened in the following ways: retention of the violence and the horror; addition of the lynching scene and of the story of Popeye's heritage; the direct and early presentation of the story of Temple and Gowan at the Old Frenchman Place; the increase of dramatic tension by the focus on Horace as the unifying "detective" protagonist, engaged in a struggle against the forces of evil.

Gothic elements which were deleted or weakened were those not essential to the dramatic present action: Horace's meditations and memories which include his consciousness of his incestuous feelings for Narcissa and greater awareness than in the novel of his feeling for Little Belle and Ruby; his dreams of his mother, Narcissa, and Ruby; the emphasis on the Benbow and the Sartoris past as reflected in the family homes and the Sartoris portraits. In the galleys Horace's consciousness of his sexual response to all the women in his life and the four canceled passages in which he gazed at the photograph of Little Belle reduce the dramatic effect of his nausea when the images of Temple and Little Belle fused, and render the episode less convincing as a sudden traumatic revelation.

Horace's active role as the detective-protagonist who links together the diverse groups of characters and their settings is greatly strengthened by the revisions, which include the rearrangement of narrative sequences, the shift of some episodes from reminiscence to present action, and the excision of long subjective passages which develop the character of Horace beyond the requirements of his role as detective-hero and his structural function. In *Sanctuary,* the revisions, especially the addition of the lynching scene, served to make the nightmare dominate the daydream in Horace's experience.

Langford is no doubt correct in interpreting the revision of *Sanctuary* as indicating Faulkner's intention to discard Horace as a character, after trying twice, "in writing and revising *Sanctuary*," "to clarify his conception of the Horace Benbow he had created in *Sartoris*." Of course, when Langford was making his study, *Flags in the Dust* had not been published. It seems that Ben Wasson's excisions constituted a first step in Faulkner's clarification or modification of his concept of Horace: Faulkner's deletions are in harmony with those made by Wasson. In both *Absalom, Absalom!* and *Sanctuary* Faulkner's revisions heightened the original strongly Gothic effect.

Sanctuary is Faulkner's most antibourgeois novel and in some ways his least regional. It is not, as Leslie Fiedler thought, "the least mythic," on "its more conscious levels": the mythic–Gothic pattern is ironically turned upside down. *Sanctuary* retains a basic function of Gothic novels, to induce the reader to identify with the characters in their terrifying and appalling experiences. It achieves its excruciating effectiveness by the contemporary action, the naturalistic background, and the psychological characterization. Its literary merits are those proper to Gothic fiction and require no apology for or explaining away of elements that fail to fit into other conventional patterns in the novel. As Michael Millgate concluded, Faulkner did indeed, in his own terms, make "a fair job" of revising the galleys of his shocking tale for publication. As a Gothic novel, *Sanctuary* is much better than "fair."

The Space between *Sanctuary*

Noel Polk

There is no need to rehearse here the details of the writing and revision of *Sanctuary;* they are well-known. What we do not know, of course, is *why* Faulkner revised it: why, having in 1929 pronounced the original version sufficiently finished for his immediate post-*Sound and Fury* standards, which were very high indeed; why, reading it in October of 1930, he found it bad enough to insist upon revising it completely, even paying part of the costs of resetting it for the privilege, so as to make of it something that "would not shame *The Sound and the Fury* and *As I Lay Dying* too much" (*Essays Speeches & Public Letters*). The question does not yield easy answers and may not, finally, yield any answers that are not too highly speculative to be useful. It is nevertheless a tantalizing and important question for the Faulkner field, because it is becoming more and more obvious that the two versions of *Sanctuary* are, like sex and death, the front and back doors to an incredible Faulknerian world that we have not yet sufficiently understood. Clearly *Sanctuary* cost him a great deal—much more, the evidence of the manuscript suggests, in the original writing than in the revising; just as clearly, the materials of *Sanctuary* were far more significant to him than his smart-aleck indictment of it—"the most horrific tale I could imagine"—allows.

Perhaps his reasons for revising were purely artistic; perhaps, on the other hand, mixed with the artistic reasons were a sufficient

From *Intertextuality in Faulkner,* edited by Michel Gresset and Noel Polk. © 1985 by the University Press of Mississippi.

number of more personal reasons, simple or complex, denied to us now because there is still a great deal we do not know about Faulkner's life during this period. We may be able, however, to understand Faulkner's need to revise *Sanctuary* by looking at the novel(s) through the curtained and opaque window Faulkner inadvertently provided for us in the work that he accomplished during the nearly eighteen months that elapsed between the two versions and by looking at the total complex of his achievement between the time of his first conception of *Sanctuary*, probably somewhere between 1925 and 1927, and the 1930 work of revising. Consider that between 1927 and 1931 Faulkner wrote *Flags in the Dust;* wrote *The Sound and the Fury;* wrote *Sanctuary;* wrote *As I Lay Dying;* revised *Sanctuary;* revised the Quentin section of *The Sound and the Fury;* and wrote and/or revised about thirty short stories, some of them among the best he would ever write. In quantity alone, this record is astounding; in quality, it is perhaps unparalleled. What he accomplished in the eighteen months between the two versions of *Sanctuary* is easily equal to what many major writers produce in a decade; it should not be too hard, then, to believe that what Faulkner taught himself about his craft during that year and a half is enough to account for his dissatisfaction with the early version.

We cannot, however, account for the two *Sanctuary*s simply by reference to chronology of composition, because in spite of a lot of factual information from this period, we still are not sure exactly when he wrote what; even if we accept strictly the order of composition indicated by dates on the manuscripts and on the short story sending schedule he kept during this period, we still cannot— or rather *I* cannot—demonstrate a straight line of artistic or thematic development from one end of the period to the other. Besides, the dates on the sending schedule could not possibly represent the order of composition; they seem rather to be the dates Faulkner recorded sending them out to magazines: even with his speed, he did not write "Mistral," "Pennsylvania Station," and "The Leg" on November 3, 1928! There is not, right now, enough evidence to prove when these and other stories were written, although it seems clear enough that many of them, at least early versions of many of them, were written in Europe or in the months immediately following his return to Mississippi.

We can, however, with some certainty trace the origins of *Sanctuary* to his time in Paris. In one letter home he described what seems to have become *Sanctuary*'s final scene: he reported having "written such a beautiful thing that I am about to bust—2000 words about the Luxembourg gardens and death," and he spoke of having done 20,000 words on his novel (in Blotner). It is not clear whether the 20,000 words and the 2,000 words are part of the same work, but it is at least possible that they are somehow related. The description of Temple Drake in the Luxembourg Gardens as it appears in *Sanctuary* (Polk's edition), however, is a mere 344 words long. Assuming that Faulkner was telling the truth, we may well ask what became of the other portions. Are they lost? Was he referring to *Elmer*? Did they become part of *Sanctuary*? Did those 20,000 or 2,000 words become part of *Flags in the Dust*, a novel with many important connections to *Sanctuary*? Even though one might persuasively argue that *Sanctuary* is at least in part an attempt to salvage some of the Benbow material Faulkner had to delete from *Flags*, it is probably more useful, finally, to think of *Flags* and *Sanctuary* as having an even more intimate, even symbiotic, relationship in their origins somewhere very early in Faulkner's career.

At least part of *Sanctuary*, then, seems to have been written before *The Sound and the Fury*, perhaps before *Flags*, perhaps even before *Soldiers' Pay* and *Mosquitoes*. Add to this possibility the fact that during the winter and spring of 1929 Faulkner revised heavily the Quentin section of *The Sound and the Fury*, and it is possible to demonstrate a close compositional relationship among *Flags*, *Sanctuary*, and *The Sound and the Fury*, that may well symbolize the degree to which all three spring from the same matrix. Further, although *Sanctuary* had been rejected by his publisher (perhaps *because* it had been rejected), much of that novel's matter—themes and images in multiple variations—found its way into short stories and into *As I Lay Dying* in ways that suggest the peculiar quality of Faulkner's imagination during the early part of the period.

What I would like to do in this essay is to look at the space between *Sanctuary*, the *Sanctuary* texts and intertexts, to speculate a bit about the differences between the two works, and to propose that the intermediate works are in fact a kind of filter through which Faulkner pushed the nightmare phantasms of *Sanctuary*, with the result, even if not the intended one, of exorcising them completely or at least of rendering them so obvious that Faulkner could—perhaps had to—suppress them. I will leave it to someone else to suggest that what Faulkner meant when he said *Sanctuary* was *bad* was that it was actually worse than bad: it was intolerably *close*.

I

The early *Sanctuary* is Horace's book entirely: his profoundest anxieties and insecurities, his deepest fears, his darkest fantasies lurk everywhere inside his tawdry, uneventful, bourgeois existence; everything that is crystallized in his relationships with all the women in his life is projected outward from his mind into the grotesque shapes of those characters from the Memphis underworld who inhabit his nightmare, for nightmare it surely is. Nearly all of *Sanctuary* takes place in darkness, in halls dimly lighted or completely dark, in houses hiding dark secrets, in tunnels formed by trees or hedges; faces appear and disappear, appear again and blur in and out of focus, and combine in crucial passages, such as the one in which Temple and Ruby and Narcissa and Horace's mother and Popeye all become one in Horace's mind. *Sanctuary*'s nightmarish qualities are an important part of its meaning. A good deal of the novel can best be understood by approaching it through the general terms laid out by Freud in his monumental study *The Interpretation of Dreams* and other works. I hasten to say that it is no purpose of mine in this essay to argue whether or how much Freud Faulkner read. There is on the one hand, of course, no known proof that he read any; there is, on the other hand, a great deal of indirect evidence that he knew much about Freud's theories. And there are a number of enigmas in *Sanctuary* that make more sense if they can be understood in terms of Freud's analyses of dreams, regardless of the degree of Faulkner's formal acquaintance with Freud's work.

That *Sanctuary* is a nightmare is rendered explicitly a number of times, nowhere more so than in the following passage, which occurs during Horace's return to Jefferson after he has been to Memphis to hear Temple's story at Miss Reba's whorehouse. He had caught the predawn train to Memphis earlier in the day; as he walks back home away from the station he has the sensation that

> there had not been any elapsed time between: the same gesture of the lighted clock-face, the same vulture-like shadows in the doorways; it might be the same morning and he had merely crossed the square, about-faced and was

returning; all between a dream filled with all the nightmare
shapes it had taken him forty-three years to invent.

All of these "nightmare shapes" become "concentrated" in the "hot,
hard lump" of undigested coffee in his stomach, which in turn
becomes the immediate physical cause of the nausea that overtakes
him only minutes later when he returns to his home and sees the
blurring face of Little Belle in the photograph. In the spectacular
conclusion to that scene, Horace vomits; and as he does so he *becomes*
Temple Drake and Little Belle: he "plunged forward and struck the
lavatory and leaned upon *his* braced arms while the shucks set up a
terrific uproar beneath *her* thighs." Likewise, the coffee he vomits,
which is something "*she* watched . . . black and furious go roaring
out of *her* pale body" (my italics), identifies him specifically with
Popeye, who to Horace smells black, "like that black stuff that ran
out of Bovary's mouth" it also connects him, not incidentally, to
other characters in the novel who vomit, Uncle Bud and Temple's
Ole Miss coed friend. Thus in the nightmare recapitulation of all that
Temple has told him, in the dreamwork's condensation of its
materials, Horace becomes Temple, Little Belle, and Popeye: he is at
one and the same time male, female, androgynous; the seducer and
the seduced; the violator and the violated; the lover and the protector;
father, brother, sister; son, lover, destroyer.

What is the source of all this? There is no clue in the 1931 text,
in which this scene survives unchanged from the early version. There
is another scene, however, cancelled in the revision, which fuels
some speculation. This is the paragraph that occurs shortly after the
beginning of chapter 12, when Horace once again passes the jail and
looks up at the window in which sit the hands of the condemned
Negro murderer. The jail window and the Negro murderer are very
important points of reference for Horace, much more important in
the first than in the revised version; the first version in fact *begins*
with the oft-noted description of that window, in which Horace sees
the Negro murderer's hands lying peacefully. Seeing them, Horace
recalls in astonishing, graphic detail the peculiarly violent nature of
the Negro's murder of his wife. We needn't be surprised that the
murder should interest Horace or that he should so strongly identify
with the murderer. Doubtless part of him admires the Negro's neat,
simple, passionate solution to his marital troubles, and perhaps in his
fantasies he wishes he were aggressive enough, masculine enough,

passionate enough, to solve his own problems so completely. Likewise, the Negro's present situation, safely incarcerated as he is in the sanctuary of the jail, is one that attracts Horace: unlike Horace, he is free of trouble and worry, free of all striving. He has nothing more troublesome to do than merely wait to die. Further, there may be in Horace's mind some relationship between the Negro murderer and Popeye—that "black man"—who is at the book's end also in jail, waiting peacefully, fretlessly, to die; it is a connection the reader cannot help making. Further still, as we shall see, Horace's complete identification with the Negro may also be a function of his feeling that he himself deserves, even wants, an appropriate punishment, from an appropriate figure, for his guilt over his murderous and incestuous fantasies, most, as nearly everybody has noted, directed toward his sister, who not for nothing is named Narcissa. In nothing is Horace more akin to Quentin Compson than in this cluster of facts and fantasies.

The passage in question was excised completely in the revision:

> Each time he passed the jail he would find himself looking up at the window, to see the hand or the wisp of tobacco smoke blowing along the sunshine. The wall was now in sunlight, the hand lying there in sunlight too, looking dingier, smaller, more tragic than ever, yet he turned his head quickly away. It was as though from that tiny clot of knuckles he was about to reconstruct an edifice upon which he would not dare to look, like an archaeologist who, from a meagre sifting of vertebrae, reconstructs a shape out of the nightmares of his own childhood, and he looked quickly away as the car went smoothly on and the jail, the shabby purlieus of the square gave way to shady lawns and houses—all the stability which he had known always—a stage upon which tragedy kept to a certain predictableness, decorum.

This is a very important passage in the early text, equally for the way it reveals the nightmare images that haunt Horace's conscious mind as for the way in which it reveals his strategies for evading all those things he doesn't want to confront directly: what he sees through that window obviously conjures up for him some childhood nightmares so powerful that he looks away immediately, self-protectively, directing his eyes and his body toward the maternal home, back toward "all the stability which he had known always."

This impulse toward evasion is in fact the pattern that begins Horace's involvement with the Memphis underworld, the underbelly of his own tepid, middle-class existence. Standing at the curtained window of his office in Kinston, looking at the "green-snared promise of unease" just outside in the ripening garden, he thinks first of the rankness of his marriage to Belle, and then, inevitably, of Little Belle: at which point he leaves the window, goes to Little Belle's room, takes her picture out of its frame, and sets out walking to Jefferson, back, ostensibly, to the security of his childhood home; he tells himself that he is counting on Narcissa's "imperviousness." Yet there is considerable evidence in the early *Sanctuary* that Horace's childhood was not by any means so serene as he remembers and that his conscious memory of that childhood as stable and secure is yet another evasion of certain truths, never directly articulated in the novel, that he does not want to face. It is precisely on the way home that all his nightmares in fact come to life: in the reflecting waters of that mysterious pond, just away from the road, kneeling, a twentieth-century Narcissus, Horace comes face to face with all the conflicting elements that compose his inner life. Popeye, whose face merges with his in the water, and at whom he stares, petrified with fright, or fascination, for two hours, is much more Horace's double than has generally been allowed: he is at once Horace's twin, his alter ego, at the same time his id and his superego; he is at once the reductio ad absurdum of Horace's darker sexual impulses as well as the punishing, vengeful father.

Again, one could ask, what is the source of all this? There is yet another significant scene in the first version, deleted in revision, which may help us understand Horace in these passages. The scene occurs in chapter 5 of the early text. Horace leaves the Sartoris household where his sister and Miss Jenny live, returns to Jefferson determined to open up their childhood home, the house where he and Narcissa grew up, and on which he has secretly paid the taxes for the past ten years. He approaches the old house through a "fence massed with honeysuckle," an association with Quentin Compson we cannot miss; he walks over a lawn whose "uncut grass" has gone "rankly and lustily to seed." As he wanders about the yard he feels it as a "tight and inscrutable desolation"—desolation, significantly, in the midst of all that suffocating fecundity—in which he moves "in a prolonged orgasm of sentimental loneliness." The house hardly inspires in him the serenity and stability he thinks he has always known there; quite the contrary. He seems to "hurdle time and surprise his sister and himself in a thousand forgotten pictures out of the serene fury of their childhood." He examines the windows of the house, which have remained exactly "as he had nailed them up ten years ago":

> The nails were clumsily driven. . . . Rusted, mute, the warped and battered heads emerged from the wood or lay hammered flat into it by clumsy blows. From each one depended a small rusty stain, like a dried tear or a drop of blood; he touched them, drawing his finger across the abrasions. "I crucified more than me, then," he said aloud.

He pulls the nails with a hammer, opens the shutter, to let in light and, going from room to room, discovers his conscious past, a highly evocative tableau, his invalid mother at the center of it:

> It seemed to him that he came upon himself and his sister, upon their father and mother, who had been an invalid so long that the one picture of her he retained was two frail arms rising from a soft falling of lace, moving delicately to an interminable manipulation of colored silk, in fading familiar gestures in the instant between darkness and sunlight.

We are unquestionably being directed to take those tightly nailed windows as eyes, symbolically nailed tightly shut upon something, some traumatic scene, some pain, particular or general, associated with Horace's childhood in this house, which he has suppressed from his memory; clearly he has seen something that has traumatized him, filled him not just with fear but also with disgust and self-loathing. Exactly what he has seen we are never told, but given Horace's obsessions as they manifest themselves throughout the book, it seems clearly to be something sexual and just as clearly to have happened at home: I propose, simply, that Horace has been traumatized by what Freud called the "primal scene," or some variation of it. There are an arresting number of similarities between *Sanctuary* and Freud's "Wolf Man" case history, which is his analysis of a young man who as a child had dreamed of waking in the middle of the night to see the window of his room open suddenly and inexplicably and reveal to his eyes a tree in which five white wolves were sitting, staring at him. Under analysis, the Wolf Man reveals that as a child he had awakened from sleep in his crib to see his father and mother engaged in what appeared to be anal intercourse—that is, his mother on her hands and knees and his father behind her. The child's immediate response was to defecate, in his bed. His long-range response was to suppress the incident entirely, both what he saw and what he did; but the incident emerged, fighting its way past the mind's censorious guards, transformed into something acceptable to, even while it troubled, the conscious mind. From the patient's childhood dream of the staring wolves, Freud builds an analytical edifice that involves the young man's family in ways that ring all sorts of bells for the reader of Faulkner—a mother in ill health, a depressed and frequently absent father, an older, dominating sister who as a child initiates him into children's sexual curiosity; further, the analysis establishes the Wolf Man's guilt over what he has seen, his shame over his defecation, his incestuous desire to have his father make anal love to him, and his simultaneous desire to be punished by his father for his sin. When he becomes Temple Drake, Horace fulfills his own rape fantasy; and it may be, finally, that Horace's and Uncle Bud's and Temple's coed friend's vomiting, as well as Temple's obsession with urination and defecation at the Old Frenchman Place, can be understood only by reference to the Wolf Man.

Horace's nightmare does not, of course, take the form of such a static visual tableau. He does not see through his window a set of white wolves; through his office window in Kinston he sees and smells the rife, fecund, suffocating, honeysuckled world of his own garden; as he continues watching through that window, the window to his own inner life, that same garden turns into the foul, rank, overgrown jungle that surrounds the Old Frenchman Place where, in the corn*crib,* Temple, his female self, is violated by Popeye as, in Temple's mind, blind Pap looks on. Horace's dream, then, substituting and transforming and inverting the actual experience, manufactures out of whatever he saw, whatever he felt, whatever he is suppressing, a world of dark fantastic characters and shapes that correspond to something in his hidden life. It is a fantastic world indeed, full of dark places and bizarre, grotesque shapes, which make the imagination of Quentin Compson seem, by comparison, a clean, well-lighted place.

There are two more scenes, one deleted from, one retained in, the revised text, which together support if they do not absolutely confirm such speculations about Horace's childhood trauma, whatever it was, and perhaps provide a base upon which we can build some generalizations about mothers and windows and doors and children and sex in Faulkner's work of this period. The first scene occurs in both versions. It is the wonderfully funny, if grotesque, scene at Miss Reba's, after Red's funeral, when Miss Reba and the two visiting madames indulge themselves in a bit of socializing; they sit around swilling beer and gin and talking about Red, Temple, and Popeye. Overhearing this conversation is the pathetic, lonely little boy, Uncle Bud, already practically an alcoholic, whose central form of amusement appears to be snitching drinks on the sly from the ladies. The madames are of course talking shop, discussing sex: normal sex, abnormal, voyeurism, and monkey glands. During their conversation Uncle Bud moves about "aimlessly" to the window where, like Horace Benbow in other passages, he peers out "beneath the lifted shade." A few pages later, after more talk of drinking and sex, the ladies become aware that Uncle Bud has gotten drunk: exasperated, Miss Myrtle "grasp[s] the boy by the arm and snatch[es] him out from behind Miss Reba's chair and [shakes] him. . . . 'Aint you ashamed? Aint you *ashamed?*' " she screams at him: "Now, you go over there by that window and stay there, you hear?" In this rather carefully executed scene, shame and windows are thus associated, the association emphasized by the fact that the word "ashamed" occurs half a dozen times in this scene, the only scene in the novel where the word is used.

The scene ends with Uncle Bud's vomiting, an act which, as we have already suggested, may serve to connect him directly to Horace; given other associations between the two, we may also be being invited to see the whole episode, which otherwise seems to be significantly outside the central narrative of the novel, as a kind of parable of Horace's childhood, if not actually a dream's distorted re-presentation of it.

If we can accept the scene as in some way rendering an episode in Horace's childhood or at least as crystallizing some quality, some essence, of that childhood; if we can entertain this notion, it becomes very tempting to see Miss Reba, by the same token, as a dreamwork version of Horace's mother. There are several reasons for suggesting this. In the early version, but not in the revision, for example,

Faulkner may have intended to associate Miss Reba and Horace's mother more directly through the specific terms of a curious tree in the yard of the old Benbow house, scene of many of Horace's fondest recollections. The tree is

> old and thick and squat, impenetrable to sun or rain. It was circled by a crude wooden bench, onto the planks of which the bole, like breasts of that pneumatic constancy so remote from lungs as to be untroubled by breath, had croached and over-bosomed until supporting trestles were no longer necessary.

Is this the self-sufficient mother, all-powerful, all-maternal, not needing the support of husband or of anybody else? It is clearly a maternal tree and may suggest that Horace was mothered to death as a child; this is, not incidentally, what Narcissa seems well on her way to doing to her son; and it is what Horace thinks Ruby is doing to her child when he accuses her of holding it too much, though the reader of the revised text only cannot understand *why* Horace thinks this. Later, in chapter 13, the fat, wheezing, constantly breathless Miss Reba is described as having huge billowing breasts, a bosom of "rich pneumasis": she moves through the room with the two dogs "moiling underfoot" like playful children and talks in a "harsh, expiring, maternal voice." Further, if as we have suggested in Horace's nightmare Popeye is Horace's father—the judge, the respectable family man become, by the substitution and inversion of the dreamwork, the impotent voyeur, the outlaw, the bootlegger, but still the punishing, vengeful father who in the dream kills the son for the Oedipal consummation; if Popeye is by inversion and repression and substitution, Horace's father, it is not at all too much to consider that Miss Reba is, by the same process of inversion and substitution, Horace's mother: the frail, lifeless, shallow-breathing invalid mother become the robust, breathless, dominating madame of a brothel. This is a substitution that both hides and symbolically reveals exactly those attributes of his mother he wants to block from his memory—precisely that world, that is, upon which he nailed those windows shut, for the sake of those more pleasant memories he wants to retain of his childhood.

The equation—Popeye-Father, Miss Reba-Mother—is not, however, quite so simple or as simplistic as it would seem, for there is another scene in the original version, deleted in revision, in which

Horace's mother, his sister, his wife, Ruby—all the objects of his sexual fantasies—and Popeye, who with the women represents Horace's failed masculinity, become fused, condensed in his imagination into one horrifying, repulsive image. Sleeping alone in the family house one night, he wakes up suddenly; the scene evokes Freud's Wolf Man:

> On the second night he dreamed that he was a boy again and waked himself crying in a paroxysm of homesickness like that of a child away from home at night, alone in a strange room. It seemed to him that not only the past two days, but the last thirty-five years had been a dream, and he waked himself calling his mother's name in a paroxysm of terror and grief. . . .
>
> After a while he could not tell whether he were awake or not. He could still sense a faint motion of curtains in the dark window and the garden smells, but he was talking to his mother too, who had been dead thirty years. She had been an invalid, but now she was well; she seemed to emanate that abounding serenity as of earth which his sister had done since her marriage and the birth of her child, and she sat on the side of the bed, talking to him. With her hands, her touch, because he realised that she had not opened her mouth. Then he saw that she wore a shapeless garment of faded calico and that Belle's rich, full mouth burned sullenly out of the halflight, and he knew that she was about to open her mouth and he tried to scream at her, to clap his hand to her mouth. But it was too late. He saw her mouth open; a thick, black liquid welled in a bursting bubble that splayed out upon her fading chin and the sun was shining on his face and he was thinking He smells black. He smells like that black stuff that ran out of Bovary's mouth when they raised her head.

Thus Horace's repression of *something* connected with aggression and sex and death and disgust and his mother is made explicit; it is not unreasonable, then, to think that Horace's mother may have been much more closely akin to Caroline Compson than to the frail, wraithlike woman he insists upon remembering. Given many other relationships between Horace and Quentin Compson, and between the novels in which they appear, we might look backward to the relationship between Caroline and Jason Compson for some sense of the nature of Horace's parents' relationship and of their effect on their children. Indeed, if John T. Irwin wanted some real doubling and incest, some real repetition and revenge, he might well have explored the Horace/Quentin relationship in *The Sound and the Fury* and the original *Sanctuary,* which seem to me far more intimately related than *The Sound and the Fury* and *Absalom, Absalom!* (*Doubling and Incest, Repetition and Revenge*).

Sanctuary drips with windows and doors, houses in which dark secrets are darkly hidden, where relationships between parents and between parents and children are founded upon suspicion and domination and sexual repression. In the early *Sanctuary,* as in *The Sound and the Fury,* as, indeed, in *Mosquitoes* and *Soldiers' Pay,* in *As I Lay Dying* and in a great deal of the short fiction of the mid- to late-twenties, sex and death and women are indissolubly associated; and Horace is, no less than Quentin Compson, no less than the entire Bundren family, no less than many other of Faulkner's protagonists of this period, simply overwhelmed by an invalid mother—this image rises screaming, insistent and peremptory, out of Faulkner's work of the twenties, and it will be worth a brief digression here to reflect on this fact.

Over and over again throughout Faulkner's work there are significant mothers: in the early years mothers who dominate and oppress—Mrs. Compson, the redoubtable Mrs. Bland, Addie Bundren, perhaps Horace's mother, certainly Narcissa; in the middle years are mothers, beginning as early as Caddy Compson, the very heart's darling herself, who abandon their children—Caddy, Dewey Dell Bundren (who wants to abandon it before it is even born), Laverne Schumann, Charlotte Rittenmeyer; in the later years this image gives way to mothers like the more ambivalent Temple Drake Stevens of *Requiem for a Nun* who, whatever else can be said about her, at least doesn't plan to abandon her *infant* child when she runs off with Pete and does plan to leave her older child with its father, who she knows will care for him; and in *The Town* there are Eula Varner Snopes, who literally sacrifices herself for her child, and Maggie Mallison Stevens, probably the healthiest, sanest, most good-humored, most *normal* female in all of Faulkner's work.

By contrast, fathers play a relatively minor role in the fiction. They are mostly weak, impotent, henpecked, peripheral, frequently absent and/or replaced by surrogate grandfathers, uncles, or older cousins. I do not forget strong fathers like Temple Drake's, or John Sartoris of *The Unvanquished,* or the foster father Simon McEachern or the fanatical Old Doc Hines in *Light in August;* nor do I forget Thomas Sutpen himself. Fathers are thus either weak unto despair, or strong unto destruction, or both, and it may be significant that there is, finally, no father in all of Faulkner, early or late, to match the heroic strength of Eula Varner Snopes or the healthy normality of Maggie Mallison. It may or may not be significant that Faulkner did not have much respect for his own father, who died in 1932; by the same token, it may or may not be significant that Faulkner's mother lived almost as long as Faulkner did and that he was clearly devoted to her, although Jay Martin has recently argued that under the surface of that relationship all was not so calm as that devotion might indicate.

II

After Smith rejected *Sanctuary,* Faulkner was left holding not just an unpublished novel, but a whole world which he apparently could not exorcise, a myriad of images that he remained preoccupied with, or at least continued to use almost compulsively, perhaps for reasons he himself did not completely understand, in the months that followed. I can best suggest the relationship of the original *Sanctuary* to the works radiating outward from it by pointing, in closing, to a connection with *As I Lay Dying.* The occasion for the connection is the following amazing passage, which occurs in both versions of *Sanctuary.* In it Temple describes to Horace Benbow part of her experience at the Old Frenchman Place:

> I hadn't breathed in a long time. So I thought I was dead.
> . . . I could see myself in the coffin. I looked sweet—you know: all in white. I had on a veil like a bride.

Then she describes her reaction to Popeye:

> I'd lie there with the shucks laughing at me and me jerking away in front of his hand and I'd think what I'd say to him. I'd talk to him like the teacher does in school, and then I was a teacher in school and it was a little black thing like a nigger boy, kind of, and I was the teacher. Because I'd say How old am I? and I'd say I'm forty-five years old. I

had iron-gray hair and spectacles and I was all big up here like women get. . . . And I was telling it what I'd do, and it kind of drawing up and drawing up like it could already see the switch.

Thus Temple, repressed, or at least unpublished, in her first appearance, becomes Addie Bundren—though to what extent this character became Addie Bundren *because* she was repressed in her Temple Drake avatar we probably will never know. But the other terms Temple uses to describe the self she creates in her fantasy extends the first *Sanctuary*'s connection to other works of the period: she has both the large maternal bosom of Miss Reba and of the tree in the Benbow yard, and the sinister iron-gray hair of the numerous repressive and repressed women in the fiction of this period. Perhaps in this latter detail we are most suggestively reminded of the remains of Emily Grierson's murderous yet withal pathetic and frustrated love for Homer Barron: the speck of iron-gray hair left on the pillow beside his skeleton.

The image of the gray-haired old woman, repressing or repressed, or both, appears throughout the fiction of this period in various combinations with windows in which their peering faces are framed or with pillows out of which their sallow faces stare, dominant. From that central image are splayed out in all directions significant connections to recurrent symbols, which may themselves come directly from Freud: windows, doors, stairs, curtains, veils, and eyes, all appearing in the service of the dominant themes of sexual frustration and impotence, and the sickness begotten of the fear of sexual experience. Note, for example, Miss Zilphia Gant's mother, and then Miss Zilphia herself, looking out of their small house through barred windows at the playground/prison outside; Miss Emily Grierson with her face framed by the window in which she constantly sits looking out at Jefferson's passing life; the white-haired mothers and grandmothers in "Ellie" and "The Brooch" who dominate their children from their bedrooms; Minnie Cooper in "Dry September" has been victimized by an invalid mother; even Miss Jenny, in "There Was a Queen," gray-haired and wheelchaired, invalided by age, watches the peculiarly "manless" Sartoris world through a window: the significance of the image for the entire period may be indicated by the fact that it supplied Faulkner an early title for this important story: "Through the Window."

The novels and stories of 1927–31 thus form a veritable spider's web of intimate connections, a fascinating web, if you will, of intertexts: touch the web at one point and you send thrilling little vibrations into nearly all the other parts.

When Faulkner found himself confronted, unexpectedly, if we may believe him, with the *Sanctuary* galleys in the fall of 1930, we may surmise that at least part of what he was dissatisfied with was that it did not reflect his current concerns—one might say his current obsessions, whatever their sources. He found himself stuck with a throwback, felt obliged not only to bring it in line with his current interests, but perhaps, consciously or unconsciously, to repress much of that portion of his earlier self, both his artistic and his personal self, that he saw reflected in that early version.

By the time he received those galleys, he had worked his way through, out of, those images and themes that occur in the space around the early *Sanctuary* with such compulsive regularity. By the fall of 1930 they seem to have been brought under some control, to have lost some of their urgency, if not to have disappeared completely. That is, the differences between the early *Sanctuary* and *Light in August* may be traceable to the differences between such intense, internalized stories of repression and frustration as "Ellie" and "A Rose for Emily" at the early end of the period and, at the late end, such stories as "Lizards in Jamshyd's Courtyard," "Red Leaves," and "Mountain Victory," for example, which, whatever one thinks of their relative quality, can at least be recognized as less sexually intense, more open, more spacious, more external in their focus than the earlier stories.

What Faulkner did to *Sanctuary* was precisely to cut or alter those passages that call attention too explicitly to Horace's childhood, his incestuous fantasies, his parents, his nightmare, and his relationship to Popeye. We are in the revision taken directly, as quickly and efficiently as possible, out of Horace's cloyingly introspective mind; what is rendered as stream of consciousness in the first version is often recast as direct quotations from Horace's conscious mind. In the first version of the scene at the pond, for example, we first see Popeye from Horace's point of view; in the revised version we rather see Horace through Popeye's eyes. From being "Horace" or "Benbow" in the first version of the scene, he becomes "the man" in the second. Finally, it is very much worth noting that while deleting all this material about Horace's background, his childhood, and his parents, the one extended passage Faulkner added to the revision was about Popeye's childhood, his background: it is a short biography in which we learn about his itinerant absent father, his "invalid" mother, and his crazy, pyromaniac grandmother. This addition is strictly in keeping with Faulkner's other efforts to put Horace at some distance from the reader and, perhaps, from himself; in this passage he simply transfers the essence of Horace's childhood directly into Popeye's: there, at least, it *seems* more appropriate.

III

I do not know whether from observations like these one can conclude anything about Faulkner's reasons for revising *Sanctuary*: whether his reasons were personal or artistic, the extent to which they represent a conscious or unconscious repression of some very significant material. The psycho-biographer might argue that Faulkner meant a great deal more than he knew when he wrote that he didn't want *Sanctuary* to "shame" *The Sound and the Fury* and *As I Lay Dying;* he might and doubtless now will pursue the possibility that many of Horace's nightmares, and some of his background, were very close to Faulkner's own and that, seeing his own traumas so baldly, so clear and unveiled through the open window of those galleys, Faulkner had, consciously or unconsciously, to suppress them. The New Critic may well argue that the revised *Sanctuary* is a "better" work of art than the early one; there is much to support such a position. I will not fuel either argument here. What I will assert, however, is that the first *Sanctuary* is, at least for the time being, in so many ways a more interesting book than the second, and that taken together, in their inter- and intratextual relationships with each other and with the other novels and stories in the space between, the two versions form a single literary text that is far more significant than either of the versions taken singly. We cannot now, I believe, pretend to understand either *Sanctuary* without also coming to terms with the other. And it seems to me obvious that there are ways in which all the texts of these years form a single intertext which holds important meanings for the study of Faulkner's work. The space between *Sanctuary* is filled with an entire teeming, fecund, even honeysuckled Faulknerian world that perhaps only these intertextual relationships can give us access to.

Desire and Despair:
Temple Drake's Self-Victimization

Robert R. Moore

Temple Drake's story has shocked, titillated, and provoked the indignation of *Sanctuary*'s readers since its 1931 publication. From the opening scenes of her girlish coquetry, through her night of terror at the Old Frenchman Place, her rape, and her apparently willing (even enthusiastic) collusion with evil at Miss Reba's and in the Goodwin trial perjury, readers respond to Temple with a complex mixture of arousal, sympathy, horror, and finally, disgust. By the end of the novel she appears no longer victim but rather, in words of one critic [William R. Brown], a "representative of a spiritually impotent society." As she sits amid the silken decadence of Miss Reba's Memphis whorehouse retelling to Horace Benbow the story of her night at the Old Frenchman Place, "in one of those bright, chatty monologues which women can carry on when they realise that they have the center of the stage," Temple seems almost to relish the texture of the experience and the effect of the telling on her audience. Her attitude is unexpected, inappropriate for a young girl so brutalized. George Toles, explaining Horace's response to Temple's manner, speaks for many readers as well: "What Temple communicates to Horace is something he would prefer not to comprehend: how she has managed to avoid being victimized in any way which would permit feelings of outrage, or even honest sympathy, to emerge. Horace is defrauded of the emotional response

From *Faulkner and Women: Faulkner and Yoknapatawpha*, edited by Doreen Fowler and Ann J. Abadie. © 1986 by the University Press of Mississippi.

which he felt was necessary to draw the perpetrated evil back somehow into an intelligible sphere of humanity." "Defrauded" of his ability to feel sympathy for Temple, Horace concludes that she—all of them—would be better off dead: "Better for her if she were dead tonight, Horace thought, walking on. For me, too. . . . all put into a single chamber, bare, lethal, immediate and profound." To Horace, Temple's response exemplifies the pervasiveness of evil as he has come to understand it. To many readers, Temple has revealed what they always suspected to be her true nature. She, more than Popeye, becomes Faulkner's intended representative of evil, one critic [Brown] goes so far as to argue.

But Faulkner is less interested in *Sanctuary,* I would suggest, with evil as a static reality than he is in how evil comes about. By the end of the novel, Temple Drake *is* part of the evil from which there is no sanctuary. Certainly, the girl who gives testimony at Goodwin's trial and who gazes vainly into her compact mirror in the Luxembourg Gardens was potentially present in the young flirt who taunted the watching town boys at the college dance. She is, nonetheless, a victim of evil as well. The process by which victim becomes victimizer is the story Faulkner tells in *Sanctuary.* Temple's unexpected, inappropriate behavior is not the enigma it has too often been made out to be. It is, instead, a key to understanding Faulkner's vision of evil.

Faulkner creates his most discomfiting effects using the symbolic imagery of defilement. Temple is touched, tainted, stained, violated by an evil which is positive, external, and infecting in the most literal sense. Paul Ricoeur, in *The Symbolism of Evil,* observes that the symbolism of defilement retains its strongest impact today in its association with illicit sexuality; and, certainly, Faulkner uses Temple's rape to evoke in his readers powerful emotional responses. The sudden awareness that comes with Eustace Graham's presentation of the bloodstained corncob at Goodwin's trial elicits our revulsion. We feel in some way soiled ourselves; and it is, perhaps, this ability of the book to affect us on a subrational level that explains the moral indignation with which *Sanctuary* has been greeted.

Dominated by images of impurity—stain, disease, contamination, dirtiness—the expression of defilement identifies evil as external. One is made impure when touched by evil; consequently, evil is initially separate from self. Images of defilement are accompanied by multiple interdictions, "thou shalt nots," conceived to restrict the possibilities of potentially corrupting experiences. There attends, then, some sense that if one is tainted by contact with evil, it is because one has violated the interdictions. More than a simple contagion in its implication of moral corruption, defilement possesses something of the power of literal disease to create fear and horror. Evil is tied to active sexuality which, in turn, is associated with outward stain (prostitutes, for example, have been called "painted women" as if they bear the outward sign of their defilement in the make-up they wear) and inward, consuming disease.

In Temple Drake, Faulkner has created the archetypal ingenue, exuding a dewy innocence, magically attractive to men, yet possessing that instinctually manipulative quality Faulkner finds characteristic of women. To her father and brothers, she is the "temple" her name implies, an object of worship, a fleshless principle to be protected. Any association, however, of this Temple with a life removed from the temptations of the flesh does not take into account the girl we first meet at the college dance. She is not the ideal Southern lady, no vestal virgin in unsullied white. She will not allow herself to be frozen on anyone's pedestal, escaping at every opportunity to play with boys who would be men, becoming the saucy flirt with "bold painted mouth" and eyes "cool, predatory and discreet." She violates the community's "thou shalt nots," sneaking out at night to ride in the town boys' cars or on the weekends to dance and party with Gowan Stevens. She enjoys the game—for to Temple, before her experience at the Old Frenchman Place, such flirting is only a game with its own rules and without heavy moral implications.

We find ourselves on a roller coaster ride of ambivalence as we respond to Temple. If she demands our sympathy and protective impulses, she is also fair game for our sexual fantasies. Faulkner captures this paradox in the casual conversation of the drummers after Goodwin's trial has ended:

> "They're going to let him get away with it, are they?" a drummer said. "With that corn-cob? What kind of folks have you got here? What does it take to make you folks mad?"
>
> "He wouldn't a never a got a trial, in my town," a second said.
>
> "To jail, even," a third said. "Who was she?"

"College girl. Good looker. Didn't you see her?"
"I saw her. She was some baby. Jeez. I wouldn't have used no cob."

Like the town, we respond to Temple both as virgin and whore; our horror at what befalls her mingles with an undefinable, leering attraction. We are disgusted and fascinated as we watch the process of Temple's degradation, seeing her as an ambiguous participant in her own debasement. We want to turn away from what we see and we want to see more.

Until the violent act of the rape, in fact, our watching her becomes a metaphor for Temple's defilement. Faulkner builds his atmosphere of terror not with physical acts so much as with a cloying voyeurism. He introduces Temple, even before the Old Frenchman Place episode, as an object watched and admired. Her car passes; boys watch. She meets Gowan Stevens at the train station; "overalled men chewing slowly" watch. She is desired, and possessing that flattering knowledge, she controls the men around her. But at the Old Frenchman Place, the watching changes from flattering to sinister. Voyeuristic scenes accumulate. Tommy sneaks a glimpse of her thigh as she struggles with her high-heeled shoe and later that evening, as she undresses, he crouches outside her bedroom window. The next morning an unidentified figure lurks in the bushes as she seeks privacy in the absence of a bathroom. As she huddles beneath the makeshift covers of the bed provided her, Faulkner offers us a scene of layered voyeurism, repeating it three times from different points of view as if to emphasize the significance. Popeye gropes at Temple beneath her nightgown as Tommy squats within the darkened room, watching. Ruby stands just inside the door, overseeing the entire scene; and soon we become aware that Faulkner has made us, as audience, the final circle of voyeurs for this sordid tableau.

This watching creates an atmosphere of terror, both for the characters and for the reader. Voyeurism becomes more than an annoying invasion of one's privacy; it becomes the psychological equivalent of the act of rape. The self is penetrated by an undefined other, by a foreign quality which insinuates itself into the sanctity of one's being. And, like the rape itself, this voyeurism conveys a sense of defilement. To the extent that Faulkner has exposed us to ourselves as a final circle of voyeurs, he causes us to see that we participate in the defilement, that we in some sense are morally culpable here.

Significantly, watching in this world replaces talking; words, in the sense of meaningful communication, are abandoned. Faulkner presents these scenes at the Old Frenchman Place increasingly as tableaus that we *must* watch from without. He transforms the voyeurism into a palpable evil first symbolically when Temple returns to the crib:

> Her hand moved in the substance in which she lay, then she remembered the rat a second time. Her whole body surged in an involuted spurning movement that brought her to her feet in the loose hulls, so that she flung her hands out and caught herself upright, a hand on either side of the corner, her face not twelve inches from the crossbeam on which the rat crouched. For an instant they stared eye to eye, then its eyes glowed suddenly like two tiny electric bulbs and it leaped at her head just as she sprung backward, treading again on something that rolled under her foot.

The eyes confront her on her own level, blazing unnaturally as if they were lit by the fires of hell, the culmination of all those eyes that have followed her movements since she left the dance. But Faulkner now presents an aggressive rather than a passive voyeurism. When the rat leaps, the nightmare potential of evil springs into reality. What has been until this point a vague though strongly felt atmosphere of terror is given form. Temple is literally cornered. The rat serves well as a symbolic agent of defilement, triggering associations with disease and filth. We experience Temple's violation here *before* the rape. Faulkner milks the scene for its melodramatic potential even to the gratuitous gesture of introducing the cob as an extraneous yet faintly menacing prop in the last line. The actual corncob rape by Popeye follows immediately; but because Faulkner chooses a radically subjective presentation which obscures the details, we do not feel the emotional terror of evil there as powerfully as we do here in the penetrating stare of the rat.

The physical acts of Tommy's murder and Temple's rape finally give evil form in the figure of Popeye, a man alienated from everything natural in the world. But the evil Faulkner presents cannot, of course, be reduced to a single character. In *Sanctuary*'s world evil is not simply present—it is pervasive. It is not simply powerful—it is omnipotent. What then is the nature of man's existence within such a world? Faulkner creates an apt metaphor for that condition as Temple sees it in the situation of the two dogs, Miss Reba and Mr. Binford, which cower beneath her bed at the Memphis whorehouse: "She thought of them, woolly, shapeless; savage, petulant, spoiled, the flatulent monotony of their sheltered lives snatched up without warning by an incomprehensible moment of terror and fear of bodily annihilation at the very hands which symbolized by ordinary the licensed tranquillity of their lives." The insidious quality of evil's threat lives not only in its physical action but also in the "terror and fear" generated by the uncertainty of the "without warning" and the arbitrariness of "the very hands." Temple interprets the dog's condition as emblematic of her own. She sees men, who under normal circumstances have represented and secured the "licensed tranquillity" of her life, as responsible for her present state, which is, in a very real sense, "incomprehensible" to her. In learning she cannot control men as she has been accustomed to doing, she feels she has also lost control over her own life. The analogy extends even further than Temple is willing to consider. This pervasive, omnipotent, arbitrary threat reduces the two dogs to snarling, snapping, thoroughly repulsive animals that command not our pity but our disgust. So, too, Faulkner seems to imply, man is diminished by his fear as much as by his actual contact with evil. The menace that stalks Temple at the Old Frenchman Place, like the threat to the dogs, is real; but its power to reduce Temple derives as much from its uncertainty and its potential as from its actuality.

So, just as the two dogs cringe in the shadows under Temple's bed in an attempt to escape their fate, Faulkner depicts his characters scrambling for refuge—sanctuary—from the crushing presence of evil. Once they become aware that evil is a real and active possibility in their world, they react immediately by trying to erect walls in the hope that they might keep this force from visiting them personally. Frantically and futilely they search for asylums, physical, social, institutional, and moral. Inevitably they fail.

Faulkner allows us some distance from Temple as she scurries around by making her vision of evil that of a child, bound up with fears of the dark and of bogeymen. The shuffling appearance of Blind Pap triggers much of Temple's flight; he seems to become the object upon which she heaps all the fears she has not otherwise been able to place. Even at the moment of the rape, she visualizes not Popeye with the corncob but "the old man with the yellow clots for eyes." Popeye, Van, Lee, and Tommy, for all their rough and crude sexual overtones, finally are only men to Temple, men whom she assumes can be manipulated with girlish pleas and coquettish smiles. Still, like a child, she reserves her greatest fears for the unknown—for the impenetrable mysteries of darkness and the freak.

But Temple's search for protection is more than a physical one. She arrives at the Old Frenchman Place secure that she carries the protective mantle of social position. For all her flirting and running around after hours with town boys, she has always been Judge Drake's daughter; and when it serves her purpose, she invokes his title as another means of attempting to control others. She implies first to Popeye and then to Lee and Ruby that certain rewards or punishments will be forthcoming from her father depending upon how she is treated. However, in *Sanctuary*'s world, proper society labels Goodwin, Ruby, and Popeye, bootlegger, prostitute, and thug, and dismisses them accordingly. If they accept this system, they accept with it their low status. So these outcasts who inhabit the Old Frenchman Place have long since chosen not to be bound within the structure of this society. Alienated as they are, the rewards or punishments of the community carry little weight with them. To the extent that Popeye is the most alienated, he is also the least threatened by its power. Faulkner exposes social position with its supposed status and protection as a convenient fiction, gaining a tenuous reality only insofar as its illusion is shared. When Temple's fears begin to overwhelm her and she prays, not with the usual invocation to God the Father, but with an incantation to her father the judge, we have already understood that social position is no more adequate as a sanctuary from evil than all those corners and cribs she searches out.

Ironically, then, Temple is more trapped within her so-called asylums than she is protected by them. She expects evil to operate by a certain logic and erects her defenses according to those expectations, but inevitably her attention is directed the wrong way at the moment evil strikes. Faulkner confounds his readers' assumptions as well in portraying an evil which refuses to play by the rules. When Temple survives the terror of that first night at the Old Frenchman Place and awakens to a sunlit spring Sunday, we feel with her a conscious relief. Raised in the tradition of Gothic horror tales, we share her belief in evil as something that goes bump in the night. With her we relax our guard momentarily against their natural backdrop of a spring morning. The scene with the rat followed by Tommy's murder jars us into recognizing evil does not comply with our expectations.

Temple's ill-fated search for sanctuaries recalls something of the language Ricoeur associated with a second symbolic pattern, the evil of sin. Sin is pride, arrogance, or belief in self-sufficiency tied to the choice of false gods, Ricoeur explains. To sin is to violate the preeminence of God in favor of the self. Temple's inability to pray points to her ruptured relationship with God; she has made of social position a false god which confers no protection. She may see herself as one of the "elect," but her election is only within a secular world. She understands her need to be "saved," but again it is only in the physical sense. Until the moment she is raped, she retains belief in her own self-sufficiency to escape the corrupting touch of evil. Her sin is a pride which entraps her. Thus, believing she is fleeing to a haven, she makes herself captive within the crib where evil discovers her.

The climactic moment of Temple's rape is a tableau. Faulkner uses it as the central metaphor for his understanding of man's ineffectuality in protecting himself from the encroaching reality of evil. He sets the scene carefully; at Temple's request Tommy crouches just inside the bolted door of the barn watching Lee Goodwin; Lee stands in the orchard watching the barn entrance; Popeye, meanwhile, circles the barn, watching them both, climbs into the loft, and lowers himself into the crib where Temple has withdrawn for safety. Temple erects her defenses against an evil external, casting about her concentric circles of watching. But evil—Popeye—awaits at the core of her sanctuary, immune to her efforts. In this scene Faulkner captures symbolically the essence of an evil which emanates from within as well as penetrates from without. It cannot be escaped because it lurks at the heart of any sanctuary man might devise. Temple, through her experiences at the Old Frenchman Place, has awakened to the menace of an evil around her, but she has not yet understood that this evil is in some part within her as well. Nor, yet, have we as readers. It is the narrative following the scenes at the Old Frenchman Place which reveals their metaphorical significance.

With the scene of Temple's rape, Faulkner has established the physical existence of evil as external and infecting in the most primitive sense of the imagery of defilement; but he has not finished with Temple. We are to understand her as more than just the object upon which evil is visited; her behavior in the latter half of the novel helps to define evil in a more complete sense. At the same time, as we come to understand these wider dimensions of evil through the actions and words of other characters, we begin to comprehend the motivations behind the perjured testimony Temple gives at Goodwin's trial.

Once Temple leaves the Old Frenchman Place, her behavior perplexes many readers. Why does she shun the opportunities to escape Popeye for the protection of the community she so yearned for during her frantic scramblings before the rape? Why does she adapt so readily to the corrupt ease of Miss Reba's whorehouse? How can we explain the way she has accommodated herself to whatever happened back at Goodwin's? Why does she seem to take such relish in recounting to Horace Benbow the story of her night of terror? Finally, why does she condemn Lee Goodwin by her perjured testimony with so little apparent remorse? If we are to answer these questions, Faulkner demands that we become something more than voyeurs. Facts, Faulkner once wrote Malcolm Cowley, are to be regarded skeptically: "I don't care much for facts, am not much interested in them, you can't stand a fact up, you've got to prop it up, and when you move to one side a little and look at it from that angle, it's not thick enough to cast a shadow in that direction." Truth, he believed, is the product of successive speculations about facts rather than something to be discovered in the facts themselves.

We are seldom privy to Temple's consciousness, yet we have clues to her motivations. The most obvious explanation is that she is controlled by Popeye. In other words, with the violation of the rape, she loses her autonomy as a human being, becoming an extension of his will. The fear he engenders in her saps her spirit and reduces her to cowering impotence. Her speculations on the fearful insecurity of Miss Reba's dogs suggest this would be how she sees herself. But in limiting our explanation to Temple's fear of Popeye, we restrict ourselves to a vision of evil as only external, a defilement so powerful and pervasive it corrupts everything it touches.

But the representation of sin differs from that of defilement in that it is expressed as an absence rather than a presence. To have sinned is to be nothing; the sinner is said to be alienated from God and from himself. "Sin makes [you] incomprehensible to [yourself],"

Ricoeur explains. Mankind is said to be lost in sin. Signified most powerfully by the slavery of the Hebrews in Egypt, the cosmic idea of sin is brought into historical context to depict the human condition under the influence of evil. The symbolic pattern is that of captivity:

> The sinner is "in" sin as the Hebrew was "in" bondage, and sin is thus an evil "in which" man is caught . . . it is a power which binds man, hardens him, and holds him captive; and it is this experience of the impotence of captivity that makes possible a taking over of the theme of defilement. However "internal" to the heart the principle of this bondage may be, the bondage in fact constitutes an enveloping situation . . . and so something of unclean contact is retained in this idea of the "captivity" of sin.

If man is passive and impotent within this representation of evil as a captive condition, it is because he recognizes that he is in some sense possessed by an inclination toward evil. God seems to have cosigned man to evil by creating him with an unmanageable will. One's desires become almost an instinct for evil action. Man is at once caught in sin and the initiator of sin through his uncontrollable will. Evil is once more a palpable, external reality, but now there is a suggestion of man's responsibility for its existence.

When Temple leaves the Old Frenchman Place, the character of her search for sanctuary changes. She is no longer fleeing a threat from without. Now she is passive, withdrawing from the so-called good people, seeking refuge from the prying eyes of the community she has left behind. When Popeye stops for food on the way to Memphis, Temple bolts from the car, not to escape from Popeye, but because she fears she might be seen by a boy she has known at school. She makes no attempt to reach her father or brothers though she can get to a telephone to call Red when she needs to. The boy from school, the doctor at Miss Reba's, her father and brothers all represent to Temple the world from which she came, a world in which "sin" was an abstraction the Baptist ladies concerned themselves with. She cannot escape the awareness of what has happened to her. She perceives what has happened as a stain immediately evident to anyone from that innocent world. The rape has made her "incomprehensible" to the self she has assumed herself to be; she now sees herself as caught within a state of sin, alienated from the community. This state becomes in time her new self-definition. Faulkner, in other words, initiates the process by which Temple internalizes the evil visited upon her.

Faulkner's characterization of Temple in Memphis is straight out of a grade B movie. She becomes a cheap twenties flapper, swilling gin, chain smoking, drinking and dancing at a local speakeasy until she works herself into a frenzy of sexual desire with Red. Our first impulse may be to criticize Faulkner for giving us the stereotyped "fallen woman" as the result of the interlude with Popeye on the floor of the crib. His imagination would seem to have faltered, yielding no more than this stock figure of moral melodrama if we conclude his purpose has been to show an evil so powerful and pervasive that it corrupts, absolutely, everything it touches. If, however, we see Temple's actions as reflecting feelings of guilt, Faulkner's portrayal becomes much more complex and interesting. "Man is guilty," explains Ricoeur, "as he feels himself guilty." Guilt arises from the individual's willing assumption of responsibility for acts he has come to perceive as evil. Temple seems to accept that the experience has transformed her into a whore, unfit for the company of the so-called good people of Jefferson. "That which is primary is no longer the reality of defilement," Ricoeur says in outlining the birth of the guilty conscience, "but the evil use of liberty, felt as an internal diminution of the value of the self." Faulkner has characterized her from the start as a passionate, headstrong girl, but one protected, or at least checked by the limits of the role the community has defined for one of her status. Her unruly will has carried her beyond the bounds of that community, however; and her almost instinctual flirtatiousness, reflecting desires that are part of her nature, has involved her in the violation of one of her community's most sacred interdictions. Now she feels cut off from any return to that community and partially responsible for her own isolation. She feels sinful so she abandons herself to acting as she naively supposes a "sinful woman" would act: gin-swilling, chain-smoking promiscuity. Her behavior is a sort of role-playing, a casting about for a new self-definition. This posturing also explains in part her "bright, chatty monologue" as she recounts to Horace the story of her experiences at the Old Frenchman Place. She has given herself to this new identity. There is self-contempt in what she does, for it reflects that she has submitted to an identity which treats only a part of her nature—physical desire—as if it were the whole. Seeing herself as alienated from that community she has known before, Temple adapts to Miss Reba's world, which offers a license to the exercise of desire; but, in doing so, she fans the self-consuming flames of her guilt.

Miss Reba recognizes that Temple is engaging in a kind of self-destruction: " 'I wish you'd get her down there and not let her come back. I'd find her folks myself, if I knowed how to go about it. . . . She'll be dead, or in the asylum in a year, way him and her go on up there in that room. . . . She wasn't born for this kind of life.' "

At the center of Ricoeur's circle lies despair, the consequence of which is the generation of evil. Temple murders Lee Goodwin with her false testimony as surely as if she were to shoot him with Popeye's gun. Why? Again, the most frequent explanation is that she acts from fear. Throughout her time on the stand, her eyes fix on the rear of the courtroom, and she cringes as she is led from the room by her family. Like Goodwin huddled in his cell before the trial expecting a bullet from Popeye's revolver to find its way through the barred windows, Temple, it is reasoned, seems to believe that Popeye awaits her just beyond the door. Like the two dogs at Miss Reba's, snarling and snapping in anticipation of some undeserved fate, she is reduced by the uncertainty of Popeye's avenging evil. The enormity of what she does—not simply absolving the guilty party but actually condemning a man she knows to be innocent—and the detachment with which she does it cannot be fully accounted for by this explanation, however. In the language with which he describes her actions and appearance in court, Faulkner suggests her experiences have reduced Temple to a shell: "Her face was quite pale, the two spots of rouge like paper discs pasted on her cheekbones, her mouth painted into a savage and perfect bow, also like something both symbolical and cryptic cut carefully from purple paper and pasted there." Temple appears in public for the first time since the rape, not as the innocent ingenue who left a few weeks before, but in her assumed role of "fallen woman," wearing the paint emblematic of her defilement. Faulkner describes her in abstract impressionistic terms of shapes and colors which deny her an element of humanity: "she gazed at the District Attorney, her face quite rigid, empty. From a short distance her eyes, the two spots of rouge and her mouth, were like meaningless objects in a small heart-shaped dish." She stares vacantly as if drugged, her eyes blank and lifeless. The woman Faulkner gives us in this scene is not really there; she is without substance, sleepwalking through a role she thinks expected of her. The earlier Temple is lost. She has made of herself a prisoner within her own consciousness, dead to an outside world. As her father leads her from the courtroom, she moves "in that shrinking and rapt abasement." Neither her testimony nor Lee Goodwin has any reality for her. Abject as she is, retaining no sense of self-worth, nothing she does or says can, in her eyes, matter. She has been caught within the web of despair. Her single, meaningful reality is a sense of isolation from the world she once knew—the world of her father, the judge, of her four brothers, and of the townspeople who fill the courtroom.

Temple and her father sit in the Luxembourg Gardens at the novel's end apparently oblivious to the world around them, bored with life. After the intensity of the trial and lynching scenes, Faulkner mutes the tone here. The electric tension which has permeated the atmosphere of *Sanctuary* is replaced by "a gray day, a gray summer, a gray year." No one watches Temple now; instead, she watches herself, gazing vainly into her compact mirror, a Narcissus wrapped up in her own image. As we find her here, Temple does seem finally lost, a victim of her own self-involvement. Through her story Faulkner has suggested the process by which evil begets evil. Temple has been changed by her contact with the evil that Popeye represents but also by her reaction to that contact, by her passivity, her surrendering of self to guilt and, finally, to despair. Confronted with the violence and sordidness of evil, she gives herself up to the pride that characterizes her worst nature. She isolates herself within a circle of her desires and guilt—the sanctuary of her impenetrable consciousness a prison that cuts her off from humanity.

Chronology

1897	Born William Cuthbert Falkner, in New Albany, Mississippi, on September 25; first child of Murry Falkner, then a railroad executive, and Maud Butler.
1914	Leaves school after long history as a poor student.
1916–17	Lives on fringe of student community at the University of Mississippi, Oxford.
1918	Tries to enlist in armed forces but is refused. Works in New Haven, Connecticut, for Winchester Gun factory. Changes spelling of name from "Falkner" to "Faulkner." Enlists in Canadian Air Force, but war ends while he is still in training.
1919	Returns to Oxford and enters the University of Mississippi. Writes poems that will be included in *The Marble Faun*.
1920	Leaves the university but remains in Oxford.
1921	After spending autumn in New York City, he returns to Oxford to work as postmaster.
1924	Resigns postmastership; *The Marble Faun*.
1925–26	New Orleans period, frequently in circle surrounding Sherwood Anderson. Writes *Soldiers' Pay* and *Mosquitoes*; travels to Europe and resides in Paris; returns to Oxford.
1927	Writes *Flags in the Dust*, which is rejected by publisher.
1928	Writes *The Sound and the Fury*.
1929	*Sartoris* (curtailed version of *Flags in the Dust*) published; marriage of Faulkner and Estelle Franklin on June 20; finishes *Sanctuary*; publishes *The Sound and the Fury*; begins *As I Lay Dying*.
1930	Finishes and publishes *As I Lay Dying*; revises *Sanctuary*.

1931   Birth and death in January of daughter, Alabama Faulk-
       ner; *Sanctuary* published; begins *Light in August.*
1932   Finishes *Light in August,* which is published after his
       father's death; begins first Hollywood screenwriting
       period.
1933   *A Green Bough;* daughter Jill born.
1934   *Doctor Martino and Other Stories.*
1935   *Pylon.*
1936   *Absalom, Absalom!*
1938   *The Unvanquished.*
1939   *The Wild Palms.*
1940   *The Hamlet.*
1942   *Go Down, Moses.*
1946   *The Portable Faulkner,* edited by Malcolm Cowley.
1948   *Intruder in the Dust.*
1949   *Knight's Gambit.*
1950   *Collected Stories;* Nobel Prize in literature.
1951   *Requiem for a Nun.*
1954   *A Fable;* first assignment for State Department as a
       goodwill ambassador.
1955   Travels to Japan for State Department; Pulitzer Prize for
       A Fable.
1957   *The Town.*
1959   *The Mansion.*
1960   Faulkner's mother dies.
1962   *The Reivers;* Faulkner dies in Byhalia, Mississippi, on
       July 6, from coronary occlusion.
1963   Pulitzer Prize for *The Reivers.*

Contributors

Harold Bloom, Sterling Professor of the Humanities at Yale University, is the author of *The Anxiety of Influence, Poetry and Repression*, and many other volumes of literary criticism. His forthcoming study, *Freud: Transference and Authority*, attempts a full-scale reading of all of Freud's major writings. A MacArthur Prize Fellow, he is general editor of five series of literary criticism published by Chelsea House. During 1987–88, he served as Charles Eliot Norton Professor of Poetry at Harvard University.

Joseph W. Reed, Jr., is Professor of English at Wesleyan University. He has published and edited work on Boswell and Walpole and is the author of *English Biography in the Early Nineteenth Century, Three American Originals: John Ford, William Faulkner and Charles Ives*, and *Faulkner's Narrative*.

Calvin S. Brown, author of *A Glossary of Faulkner's South*, teaches English at the University of Georgia.

Jean Weisgerber is author and editor of a two-volume series on the history and theory of modern literature, *Les Avant-Gardes Littéraires au XX Siècle*. He has also written *Faulkner and Dostoevsky: Influence and Confluence*.

Albert J. Guerard, Professor of Literature at Stanford University, is the author of *The Exiles, The Touch of Time: Myth, Memory and Self*, and *The Triumph of the Novel: Dickens, Dostoevsky, Faulkner*. He has also published studies of Conrad and Hardy, as well as seven novels, most recently *Christine-Annette* (E. P. Dutton, 1985).

Elizabeth M. Kerr, in addition to her book *William Faulkner's Gothic Domain*, has written *William Faulkner's Yoknapatawpha: "A Kind of Keystone in the Universe."*

Noel Polk, Professor of English at the University of Southern Mississippi, is an internationally recognized Faulkner scholar. He has published numerous works on Faulkner and edited *Sanctuary: The Original Text* for Random House.

Robert R. Moore teaches English at the State University of New York at Oswego, where he directs the composition program. He has written numerous articles on Faulkner's work.

Bibliography

Adams, Richard P. *Faulkner: Myth and Motion*. Princeton: Princeton University Press, 1968.

Aiken, Conrad. "William Faulkner: The Novel as Form." In *William Faulkner: Three Decades of Criticism*, edited by Frederick J. Hoffman and Olga Vickery. East Lansing: Michigan State University Press, 1960.

Asselineau, Roger. "The French Face of William Faulkner." *Tulane University Studies in English* 23 (1978): 157–73.

Backman, Melvin. *Faulkner: The Major Years, A Critical Study*. Bloomington: Indiana University Press, 1966.

Bassett, John E. *William Faulkner: The Critical Heritage*. London: Routledge & Kegan Paul, 1975.

———. "*Sanctuary:* Personal Fantasies and Social Fictions." *South Carolina Review* 14, no. 1 (Fall 1981): 73–82.

Beck, Warren. *Faulkner: Essays by Warren Beck*. Madison: University of Wisconsin Press, 1976.

Blotner, Joseph L. *Faulkner: A Biography*. 2 vols. New York: Random House, 1974.

Brooks, Cleanth. *William Faulkner: The Yoknapatawpha Country*. New Haven: Yale University Press, 1963.

———. "Faulkner's *Sanctuary:* The Discovery of Evil." *Sewanee Review* 71 (1963): 1–24.

Brown, William R. "Faulkner's Paradox in Pathology and Salvation: *Sanctuary, Light in August, Requiem for a Nun.*" *Texas Studies in Literature and Language* 9 (1967): 429–49.

Brylowski, Walter. *Faulkner's Olympian Laugh: Myth in the Novels*. Detroit: Wayne State University Press, 1968.

Campbell, Harry Modean, and Ruel E. Foster, eds. *William Faulkner: A Critical Appraisal*. Norman: University of Oklahoma Press, 1951.

Chamberlain, John. "Dostoevsky's Shadow in the Deep South." *The New York Times Book Review*, February 15, 1931, p. 9.

Cole, Douglas. "Faulkner's *Sanctuary:* Retreat from Responsibility." *Western Humanities Review* 14 (Summer 1960): 291–98.

Cowley, Malcolm. *The Faulkner-Cowley File: Letters and Memories, 1944–1962*. New York: Viking, 1966.

———. "Introduction to *The Portable Faulkner*." In *William Faulkner: Three Decades of Criticism,* edited by Frederick J. Hoffman and Olga Vickery. East Lansing: Michigan State University Press, 1960.

Creighton, Joanne V. "Self-Destructive Evil in *Sanctuary.*" *Twentieth Century Literature* 18 (1972): 259–70.

Cypher, James R. "The Tangled Sexuality of Temple Drake." *American Imago* 19 (1962): 243–52.

Esslinger, Pat M., et al. "No Spinach in *Sanctuary.*" *Modern Fiction Studies* 18 (1972–73): 555–58.

Faulkner, William. *Essays Speeches & Public Letters.* Edited by James B. Meriwether. New York: Random House, 1965.

Fiedler, Leslie. *Love and Death in the American Novel.* New York: Criterion, 1959.

Fowler, Doreen. *Faulkner's Changing Vision: From Outrage to Affirmation.* Ann Arbor, Mich.: UMI Research Press, 1983.

Fowler, Doreen, and Ann J. Abadie, eds. *Fifty Years of Yoknapatawpha: Faulkner and Yoknapatawpha, 1979.* Jackson: University Press of Mississippi, 1980.

Frazier, David L. "Gothicism in *Sanctuary:* The Black Pall and the Crap Table." *Modern Fiction Studies* 2 (1956): 114–24.

Friedman, Alan Warren. *William Faulkner.* New York: Ungar, 1984.

Frohock, W. M. *The Novel of Violence in America.* Dallas: Southern Methodist University Press, 1957.

Gresset, Michel, and Noel Polk, eds. *Intertextuality in Faulkner.* Jackson: University Press of Mississippi, 1985.

Gwynn, Frederick L., and Joseph L. Blotner, eds. *Faulkner in the University: Class Conferences at the University of Virginia, 1957–58.* New York: Random House, 1965.

Hoffman, Frederick J. *William Faulkner.* New York: Twayne, 1961.

Hoffman, Frederick J., and Olga Vickery, eds. *William Faulkner: Three Decades of Criticism.* East Lansing: Michigan State University Press, 1960.

Howe, Irving. *William Faulkner: A Critical Study.* New York: Vintage, 1962.

Howell, Elmo. "The Quality of Evil in Faulkner's *Sanctuary.*" *Tennessee Studies in Literature* 4 (1959): 99–107.

Kinney, Arthur F. *Faulkner's Narrative Poetics: Style as Vision.* Amherst: University of Massachusetts Press, 1978.

Kubie, Lawrence. "William Faulkner's *Sanctuary.*" *Saturday Review of Literature* 11 (1934): 218, 224–26.

Langford, Gerald. *Faulkner's Revision of* Sanctuary. Austin: University of Texas Press, 1972.

Lisca, Peter. "Some New Light on Faulkner's *Sanctuary.*" *Faulkner Studies* 2 (1953): 5–9.

Longley, John Lewis, Jr. *The Tragic Mask: A Study of Faulkner's Heroes.* Chapel Hill: University of North Carolina Press, 1963.

McHaney, Thomas L. "*Sanctuary* and Frazer's Slain Kings." *Mississippi Quarterly* 24 (1971): 223–45.

Magny, Claude-Edmonde. *The Age of the American Novel: The Film Aesthetic of Fiction between the Two Wars.* Translated by Eleanor Hochman. New York: Ungar, 1972.

Martin, Jay. " 'The Whole Burden of Man's History of His Impossible Heart's Desire': The Early Life of William Faulkner." *American Literature* 53 (1982): 607–29.

Mason, Robert L. "A Defense of Faulkner's *Sanctuary*." *Georgia Review* 21 (1967): 430–38.

Materassi, Mario. *I Romanzi di Faulkner*. Rome: Edizioni Abete, 1968.

Mayoux, Jean. *Vivants Piliers: Le Roman anglo-saxon et les symboles*. Paris: Julliard, 1960.

Miller, James E., Jr. "*Sanctuary:* Yoknapatawpha's Wasteland." In *Individual and Community: Variations on a Theme in American Fiction,* edited by Kenneth H. Baldwin and David K. Kirby, 137–59. Durham, N.C.: Duke University Press, 1975.

Millgate, Michael. *The Achievement of William Faulkner*. New York: Random House, 1966.

Miner, Earl. *The World of William Faulkner*. Durham, N.C.: Duke University Press, 1952.

O'Connor, William Van. *The Tangled Fire of William Faulkner*. Minneapolis: University of Minnesota Press, 1954.

O'Donnell, George Marion. "Faulkner's Mythology." In *William Faulkner: Three Decades of Criticism,* edited by Frederick J. Hoffman and Olga Vickery. East Lansing: Michigan State University Press, 1960.

Page, Sally R. *Faulkner's Women: Characterization and Meaning*. Deland, Fla.: Everett/Edwards, 1972.

Parker, Robert Dale. *Faulkner and the Novelistic Imagination*. Urbana: University of Illinois Press, 1985.

Perry, J. Douglas. "Gothic as Vortex: The Form of Horror in Capote, Faulkner, and Styron." *Modern Fiction Studies* 19 (1973): 153–67.

Pikoulis, John. *The Art of William Faulkner*. London: Macmillan, 1982.

Polk, Noel. " 'The Dungeon was Mother Herself': William Faulkner 1927–1931." In *New Directions in Faulkner Studies: Faulkner and Yoknapatawpha, 1983,* edited by Doreen Fowler and Ann J. Abadie, 61–93. Jackson: University Press of Mississippi, 1984.

———, ed. *Sanctuary: The Original Text*. New York: Random House, 1981.

Putzel, Max. *Genius of Place: William Faulkner's Triumphant Beginnings*. Baton Rouge: Louisiana State University Press, 1985.

Rossky, William. "The Pattern of Nightmare in *Sanctuary;* or, Miss Reba's Dogs." *Modern Fiction Studies* 15 (1969): 503–15.

Seyppel, Joachim. *William Faulkner*. Berlin: Colloquium Verlag, 1962.

Simpson, Lewis P. "Isaac McCaslin and Temple Drake: The Fall of New World Man." In *Nine Essays in Modern Literature,* edited by Donald E. Stanford, 88–106. Baton Rouge: Louisiana State University Press, 1965.

Slabey, Robert. "Faulkner's *Sanctuary*." *The Explicator* 21 (January 1963), item 45.

Slatoff, Walter. *Quest for Failure: A Study of William Faulkner*. Ithaca: Cornell University Press, 1960.

Stein, William Bysshe. "The Wake in Faulkner's *Sanctuary*." *MLN* 75 (1960): 28–29.

Straumann, Heinrich. *William Faulkner*. Frankfurt am Main: Athenäum Verlag, 1968.

Sundquist, Eric J. *Faulkner: The House Divided.* Baltimore: The Johns Hopkins University Press, 1983.

Swiggart, Peter. *The Art of Faulkner's Novels.* Austin: University of Texas Press, 1962.

Tate, Allen. *Memoirs and Opinions: 1926–1974.* Chicago: Swallow, 1975.

Thompson, Lawrance. *William Faulkner: An Introduction and Interpretation.* New York: Barnes & Noble, 1963.

Toles, George. "The Space Between: A Study of Faulkner's *Sanctuary.*" *Texas Studies in Literature and Language* 22 (1980): 22–47.

Urgo, Joseph R. "Temple Drake's Truthful Perjury: Rethinking Faulkner's *Sanctuary.*" *American Literature* 55 (1983): 435–44.

Vickery, Olga. *The Novels of William Faulkner.* Rev. ed. Baton Rouge: Louisiana State University Press, 1964.

Volpe, Edmund. *A Reader's Guide to William Faulkner.* New York: Farrar, Straus & Giroux, 1964.

Waggoner, Hyatt. *William Faulkner: From Jefferson to the World.* Lexington: University Press of Kentucky, 1959.

Warren, Robert Penn, ed. *Faulkner: A Collection of Critical Essays.* Englewood Cliffs, N.J.: Prentice-Hall, 1966.

Wasiolek, Edward. "Dostoevsky and *Sanctuary.*" *MLN* 74 (1959): 114–17.

Williams, David. *Faulkner's Women: The Myth and the Muse.* Montreal: McGill-Queens University Press, 1977.

Wittenberg, Judith Bryant. *Faulkner: The Transfiguration of Biography.* Lincoln: University of Nebraska Press, 1979.

Acknowledgments

"The Function of Narrative Pattern in *Sanctuary*" (originally entitled *"Sanctuary"*) by Joseph W. Reed, Jr., from *Faulkner's Narrative* by Joseph W. Reed, Jr., © 1973 by Yale University. Reprinted by permission of Yale University Press. Selections from the works of William Faulkner reprinted by permission of Random House, Inc.

"*Sanctuary:* From Confrontation to Peaceful Void" by Calvin S. Brown from *Mosaic* 7, no. 1 (Fall 1973), special issue: *The Novels of William Faulkner*, edited by R. G. Collins and Kenneth McRobbie, © 1973 by the Editors, *Mosaic.* Reprinted by permission.

"*Sanctuary* and Dostoevsky" (originally entitled "Evil and Fate: Raskolnikov [1929–1934]—*Sanctuary* [1931]") by Jean Weisgerber from *Faulkner and Dostoevsky: Influence and Confluence* by Jean Weisgerber, translated by Dean McWilliams, © 1974 by Ohio University Press. Reprinted by permission.

"*Sanctuary* and Faulkner's Misogyny" (originally entitled "Forbidden Games [III]: Faulkner—Sanctuary") by Albert J. Guerard from *The Triumph of the Novel: Dickens, Dostoevsky, Faulkner* by Albert J. Guerard, © 1976 by Albert J. Guerard. Reprinted by permission.

"*Sanctuary:* The Persecuted Maiden, or, Vice Triumphant" by Elizabeth M. Kerr from *William Faulkner's Gothic Domain* by Elizabeth M. Kerr, © 1979 by Kennikat Press Corp. Reprinted by permission of Associated Faculty Press, Inc.

"The Space between *Sanctuary*" by Noel Polk from *Intertextuality in Faulkner*, edited by Michel Gresset and Noel Polk, © 1985 by the University Press of Mississippi. Reprinted by permission.

"Desire and Despair: Temple Drake's Self-Victimization" by Robert R. Moore from *Faulkner and Women: Faulkner and Yoknapatawpha*, edited by Doreen Fowler and Ann J. Abadie, © 1986 by the University Press of Mississippi. Reprinted by permission.

Index

145

Marmeladov, Sonia (*Crime and Punishment*), 61
Martin, Jan, 116
Marx, Karl, 4
Materassi, Mario, 28, 82
Mayoux, Jean, 84, 90
Melville, Herman, 1, 65
Memphis, 16, 25, 48, 65, 77, 106; flight to, 18, 35, 94, 97; gang conflicts in, 64; as Gothic milieu, 85; the Grotto in, 85, 87; Temple Drake in, 69, 76; underworld of, 38, 48, 51, 106, 109, 131
Meursault (*The Stranger*), 66–67
Midnight, 14
Millgate, Michael, 77; *The Achievement of William Faulkner,* 81, 101
Miner, Earl, 29
Minnie, Miss, 66, 80
Minter, David, 1
Mississippi, 64, 65, 74
"Mistral," 104
Mitchell, Belle. *See* Benbow, Belle Mitchell
Mitchell, Titania, "Little Belle": and Horace, 34, 57, 58, 67–68, 76, 89, 100, 109; and Temple, 87, 90, 107
Montand, Yves, 14
Morell, Giliane, 82
Mosquitoes, 105, 115
"Mountain Victory," 118
Movies, 14, 16, 25, 78–79
Munch, Edvard, "The Scream" (painting), 82
Myrtle, Miss, 41, 42, 80, 112
Mythmaking, 2

New Criticism, 2, 119
Newgate Calendar, 14
Nietzsche, Friedrich, 1

O'Connor, William Van, 28
O'Donnell, George Marion, 27, 99
"Odor of Verbena, An," 88
Old Frenchman Place, 29, 37, 44, 49, 65, 66, 69, 73, 76, 77; blind man at, 13, 91, 97, 111, 126–27; fictional use of, 84, 85, 125; founding of, 84; free-for-all at, 40, 46; as Gothic setting, 97; and Gowan, 88, 100; Horace at, 31, 32, 34; and Temple Drake, 86, 92, 93, 111, 121, 123, 124–25, 126, 127, 128, 129, 130, 131
Oxford (Mississippi), 17, 25, 64, 94

Paradise Lost (Milton), 25
Pater, Walter, 2, 6
"Pennsylvania Station," 104
Perry, Douglas, 82–83, 92, 96; "Gothic as Vortex," 83, 98
Persephone, 84
Petrovich, Porfiry (*Crime and Punishment*), 53
Plato, 7
Pluto, 84
Pole, the (*The Brothers Karamazov*), 54
Popeye, 8, 14, 15, 16, 20, 54; apathy of, 46, 48–49, 50, 51, 52, 108; characterization of, 7, 12, 17, 24, 29, 49, 65–66, 88, 89, 90, 91; character of, and comic strip, 83; control of Temple Drake of, 129; crime of, 53, 55; as enigma, 28–29; flight from justice of, 96; flight to Memphis of, 44, 84, 97; hanging of, 9, 31, 49, 55, 66, 97; heritage of, 25, 49, 73, 100, 119; as Hermes, 29; and Horace Benbow, 6–7, 19, 29–31, 33, 34, 37, 59, 76, 89, 108, 109, 111, 118; impotence of, 66, 71, 78, 83, 87, 90, 96, 97; as instrument of evil, 29, 59, 66, 122, 125, 128, 133; and Judge Drake, 92; language of, 30; and Lee Goodwin, 37, 45, 46, 48, 86, 90, 96; and Miss Reba, 41–42, 61, 80; and Nature, 24, 25, 29, 74; rape of Temple Drake by, 56, 66, 73, 125, 128; and Red, 98; as symbol of mechanical civilization, 22, 29; and Temple Drake, 24, 35, 36, 54, 70, 72, 93, 116, 124, 132; and Tommy, 34; trial of, 48, 63; voyeurism of, 77, 80, 85, 90, 97
Pumphrey, Popeye, 83

Radcliffe, Anne, 86
Raskolnikov (*Crime and Punishment*), 53